Smuggling Days

K. Merle Chacksfield

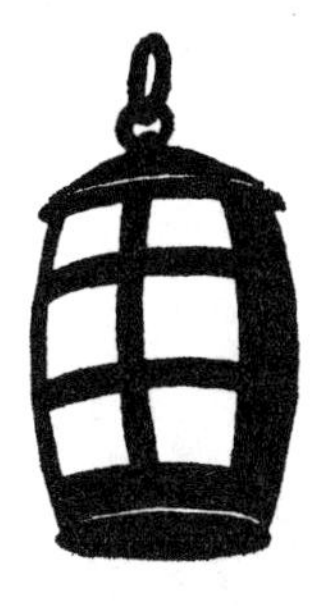

Back and front covers: cliffs at Handfast Point, Dorset, from Swanage Bay, showing chalk stacks, namely (from back to front, left to right) the principal Pinnacle, Turf Rick Rock, a smugglers' cave called Parson's Barn, No Man's Land, and the famous Old Harry.

DORSET PUBLISHING COMPANY, KNOCK-NA-CRE,
MILBORNE PORT,
SHERBORNE, DORSET DT9 5HJ

Illustrations by Robert A. Chacksfield and J.H. Lavender B.Sc, A.R.C.S.

Clarissa could well have been smuggled in from France, see page 16.

Publishing details. Third edition, revised 1984.
Printing credits. Printed in Great Britain by Wincanton Litho, Old National School, Wincanton, Somerset, and Butler and Tanner Limited of Frome, Somerset.
Distribution. Trade sales distribution by Dorset Publishing Company, from Knock-na-cre, Milborne Port, Sherborne, Dorset DT9 5HJ, telephone 0963 32583.
International Standard Book Number. (ISBN) 0 902129 56 2

"A smuggler is a wretch who, in defiance of the law, imports or exports goods without payment of the customs."

Dr. Johnson.

*　*　*　*

"A smuggler is a person who, although no doubt blameable for violating the laws of the country, is frequently incapable of violating those of natural justice, and would have been, in every respect, an excellent citizen had not the laws of his country made that a crime which Nature never meant to be so."

Adam Smith,
Philosopher and Economist, and
Son of an official in the Customs.

SMUGGLERS AT HENGISTBURY HEAD

Flood tide — and shapes in the dykes!

From the headland cloaked by night
A lantern beam shines brightly seaward,
And waiting, sails spilled, for a sign
To land her cargo, a silent ship
Stirs to life at the gleam of light.

Flood tide — and shapes in the dykes!

Muffled hooves and harness creaking,
Covered waggons — hand to hand the
Men are loading tubs of brandy
Slipped on shore from little boats
To wary landsmen, rarely speaking.

Flood tide — and shapes in the dykes!

Hidden faces do not show
The Parson, Squire or farmhand leading
Straining horses from the shore
To the inns and markets inland
Where the contraband will go.

Ebb tide — no shapes in the dykes

The headland's bare in the dawn's pale light,
Rattling pebbles in hissing surf
The only sound, with the sea-bird's call;
A silver ship with swelling sails
Heels to the breeze and steals from sight.

K. Merle Chacksfield

GLOSSARY

Gauger Gobloo Gobbie Preventer	Preventive Officer Customs and Excise Officer
Free-traders Venturers The Gentlemen	Smugglers
Run	A quick passage of contraband goods from a port in Holland, France or the Channel Islands to a landing place on the English coast.
Anker	Old Dutch measure — barrel capacity 10 gallons.
Keg	Small barrel less than 10 gallons.
Grappling Creeping	Using grappling hooks to regain cargo at the bottom of the sea, river beds or ponds.
Sweeping	Regaining goods from the sea with two boats.
Crop	Contraband Cargoes.
Stinkibus	High smelling spirits — left in the sea too long.
Sling the load	Fix ropes for carrying tubs.
Spout Lantern	A lantern with a long spout through which a beam of light was directed — usually used to signal to smugglers at sea.
Flink	A warning light to smugglers.

CONTENTS

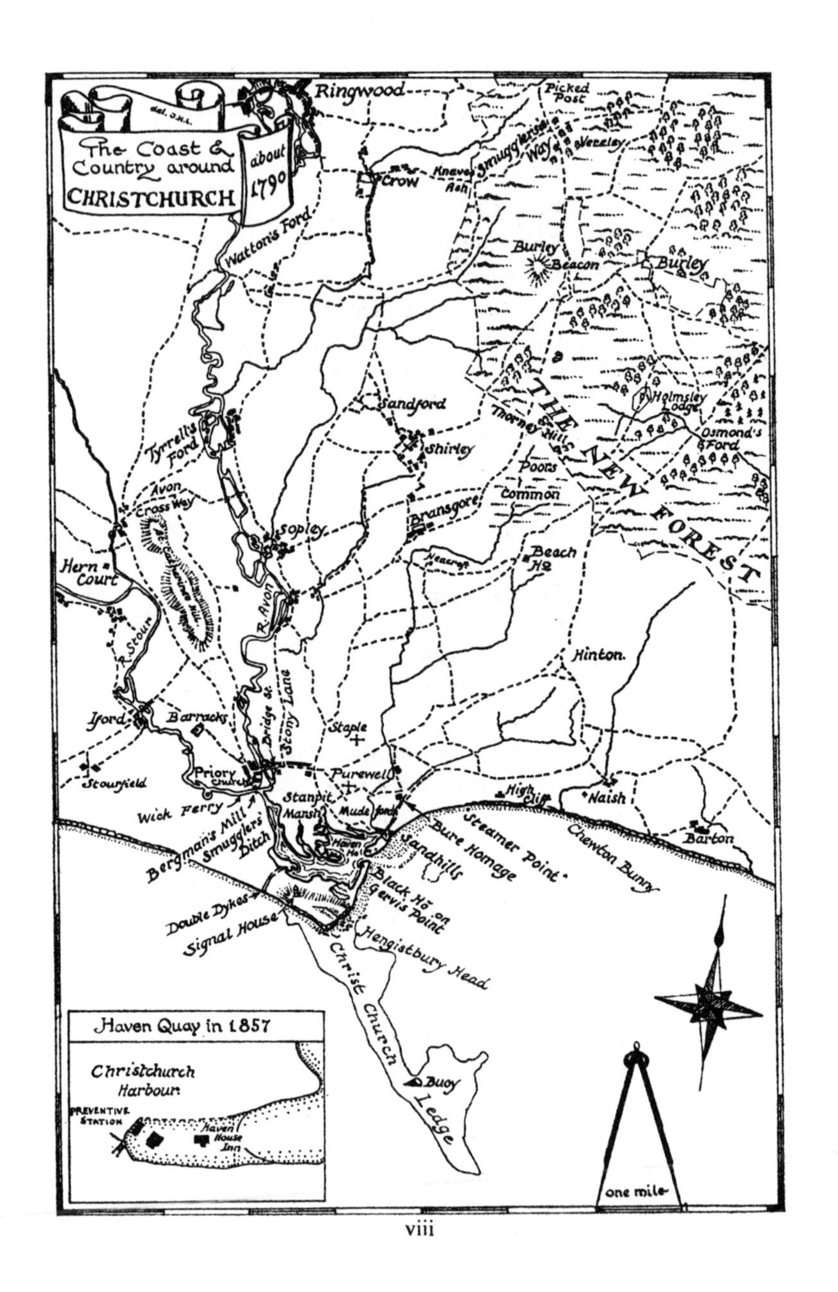
The Coast & Country around CHRISTCHURCH
about 1790
Ringwood
Picked Post
Smugglers' Way
Vereley
Crow
Kneves Ash
Wattons Ford
Burley Beacon
Burley
THE NEW FOREST
Holmsley Lodge
Osmond's Ford
Thorney Hill
Poors Common
Sandford
Shirley
Tyrrell's Ford
Avon Cross Way
Sopley
Bransgore
Neacroft
Beach Ho
Hern Court
R. Stour
R. Avon
Hinton
Iford
Barracks
Bridge St.
Stony Lane
Staple
Stourfield
Priory Church
Purewell
Wick Ferry
Bergman's Mill
Smugglers' Ditch
Stanpit Marsh
Mudeford
Haven Ho
High Cliff
Naish
Bure Homage
Steamer Point
Sandhills
Chewton Bunny
Barton
Black Ho. on Gervis Point
Double Dykes
Signal House
Hengistbury Head
Christ Church Ledge
Buoy
Haven Quay in 1857
Christchurch Harbour
PREVENTIVE STATION
Haven House Inn
one mile

Introduction

THE night was still, and darkness covered the headland like a cloak. Floodtide—and shapes in the dykes! From the clifftop a lantern flashed its message over the inky sea.

Ghostly ships slipped their dark secrets to the shore, where the pebbles rattled and slipped under the heavy feet of men who were loading tubs and kegs into covered waggons and on the saddles of horses, which impatiently scraped muffled hooves, harness creaking as the load grew heavier.

"Have a care with those tubs," snarled the chief, "or it'll be the last load you'll see, you dog!"

"Have a care, have a care!" thought Fred. "Must keep goin' for Jenny's sake."

He passed on the tubs to Will, more carefully now.

"Jenny needs the money—more'n ever. Five shillings," he mused, "an' likely there'll be more for the tubs we get past them Excise gobloos."

He glanced around.

"Is this the lot then, Will?"

"Aye. Sling your own load now, Fred," grunted the man beside him as he fastened a tub before and another behind his mighty body.

A signal from the chief and, slowly at first, the army of ten, twenty, or thirty waggons and close on a hundred men and horses left the fern-fringed dykes of Hengistbury Head and streamed past the cool harbour, making for the wild country to the north-west of Christchurch.

On they moved, unhindered, over the winding tracks of Bourne Heath. "Must've been going best part of two hours now," muttered Fred, as they pushed on the waggons to help the struggling horses heave their load up the hill.

"Aye," said Will, wiping the sweat from his eyes. " 'Tes breakin' a bit over to the east there. Time we 'ad a rest."

Fred nodded, his back aching and the tubs heavier with every step.

"There's still another field of hay to get in," he thought, wondering how he'd have the strength to swing a scythe in the daylight. "Keep goin'," his brain insisted, "not long now — not long now."

Round a bend in the road they came to an inn, and the chief halted the team while he went inside. A candlelight travelled downstairs and lit up the cheery face of the inn-keeper at the door.

"Eight tubs this time, and if you keep your mouth shut there'll be more later," muttered the chief. Four carriers unloaded their tubs, and thirty-two golden pieces were slipped into the chief's hard hands.

The leader then drove his straggling army forward again. They passed sleeping cottages, and dropped a load here at a farm, or there in the cellar of a manor house. By now, half the men had been paid off and sent home, but the rest, tired and weary, dragged on.

Suddenly a shout rang from the trees, and a lone Riding Officer confronted the party.

"Ride on, you dogs!" raged the chief, "I'll curse the man who stays."

A pistol flashed. Someone was hurt, but the chief lashed them on with his tongue, and the Riding Officer wheeled about and galloped away for help.

The murmuring, ragged, jostling band moved on, and a stumbling load of tubs suddenly crashed on Will.

"You crazy loon!" he growled. "Can't you see what . . . Why, 'tis Fred, poor old Fred!"

He put his strong hand under Fred's arm and helped him along. Fred smiled. His wounded shoulder felt less painful now, and his load lighter.

"Good old Will," he said, "I'm feelin' better already. Jenny'll be waitin' for me."

The heaving, straining army of men and horses moved on before the morning light betrayed them to the pursuing soldiers.

Later, in a small thatched cottage at the edge of the river, Fred looked down at Jenny.

" 'Tes our boy, Fred, our first baby," she said shyly, and as Fred uncurled the baby's tiny fingers and folded a gold piece in the warm little hand, he smiled.

"He's a fine child, Jenny, a fine child, an' there'll be food for us all for a while."

* * * *

So many times in the eighteenth and early nineteenth centuries must the shores of Christchurch, and, indeed the whole south coast, have witnessed such a scene, for smuggling played an important part in the economic life of the people. Tea, tobacco, silks, laces, brandy and wines were smuggled, mainly from France and the Channel Islands, to these shores, while aristocrats escaping from the French Revolution were also valuable and rewarding contraband.

The Christchurch coast, with its fine beaches and chines, or ravines, running down to the sea was ideal for the smuggler. Christchurch Harbour was certainly a haven for him, as the entrance was difficult to navigate by those who did not know its peculiarities. This was frustrating to the officers in the revenue cutters, and the men of Christchurch were well aware of its natural advantages, for they never seemed to show much interest in any dredging or improvement of the harbour.

It was not easy for the Riding Officer of Customs and Excise to patrol the coastline from Poole to Hurst Castle with a mere handful of customs officers, a few Dragoons and the help of the occasional informer, so that smuggling flourished around Christchurch and Bourne Heath for more than a hundred years after the introduction of Walpole's Excise Bill in 1733. Usually it was a spare-time occupation and a source of extra income for the labourer, the fisherman and the small tradesman, much needed in those poverty-stricken times when a labourer's wage was seven shillings a week and meat was a rare luxury.

A smuggling run was a matter of co-operation between the captain of a fast sailing vessel, who bought and transported the goods from abroad, the Venturer, a wealthy and influential citizen who financed the enterprise, the Lander, who was relied upon to receive the contraband and see it distributed to the various markets at his disposal, and the Clerk, often a bank or vestry clerk, who kept the accounts.

The whole population appeared to be on the side of the smugglers, and small wonder, for not only did they receive tea, tobacco and brandy at half price, but for trifling acts such as lending a pony or shining a light at the right time they would be rewarded with some of the contraband.

Smuggled goods found their way into homes at all levels of society, and even the parson was not always averse to a nightcap of contraband French brandy.

However, not every parson allowed himself to be comforted by this earthly spirit, and in 1778 the Revd. William Jackson, Vicar of Christchurch, who held strong views against smuggling, told his Parish Clerk that it was a grievous sin.

The Clerk replied,

"Then the Lord have mercy on the town of Christchurch, for who is there here who has not had a tub?"

Christchurch Priory Church

1

The Smugglers

FOR centuries an important matter the Government had to deal with was the illegal exportation of wool to the Continent.

The 'owlers', as the wool smugglers of the night were called, would defy death and bodily harm to ship their wool secretly from England to the Continent.

The Government had restricted the sale of wool abroad in an attempt to protect its cloth manufacturers. In fact this interference with trade led to the introduction of bad laws which enabled the cloth makers to dictate their own terms to the wool growers.

Accordingly the wool growers sometimes suffered difficulties. For example, during the reign of Edward I, export duty on a bale of wool was £12 (1967 values), and in 1660 it was forbidden to export wool at all.

Owing to the harshness of these duties the 'owlers', in association with the wool growers, practised wholesale exportation of wool from Romney Marshes, in Kent, to France and the Low Countries.

Undoubtedly, the injustice and severity of taxation enforced by successive Governments caused unrest amongst generations of citizens of this country. Smuggling was all fair enough, people would say, and there was no harm in cheating the Government, because Governments cheated you.

These conditions bred, for the most part, reckless bands of smugglers, which became highly organised during the 18th and early part of the 19th centuries.

Hardly any part of the coast was without its gang of smugglers, and every stretch of beach, and every inlet, was used as a landing place for contraband at the end of a run, which was the name given to a speedy transit of contraband from Holland, France or the Channel Islands to a predetermined rendezvous on our southern shores.

The hey-day of smuggling was during the reign of George III (1760-1820). It was a time of heavy duties and excessive taxation, and the profits from contraband were very high. In 1820 Sidney Smith warned the United States against too much taxation. He said (of England),

> "being too fond of glory there were taxes upon every article which enters into the mouth or covers the back, or is placed under the foot; taxes upon everything which is pleasant to see, hear, feel, smell, or taste; taxes upon warmth, light and locomotion; taxes on everything on earth, and the waters under the earth; on everything that comes from abroad, or is grown at home; taxes on the raw material, taxes on every fresh value that is added to it by the industry of man; taxes on the sauce which pampers man's appetite and the drug that restores him to health; on the ermine which decorates the judge and the rope which hangs the criminal; on the poor man's salt and the rich man's spice; on the brass nails of the coffin and the ribands of the bride; at bed or

board, couchant or levant, we must pay. The schoolboy whips his taxed top; the beardless youth manages his taxed horse with a taxed bridle on a taxed road; and the dying Englishman, pouring his medicine, which has paid 7%, into a spoon that has paid 15%, flings himself back on his chintz bed which has paid 22%, makes his will on an £8 stamp and expires into the arms of an apothecary who has paid a licence of £100 for the privilege of putting him to death. His whole property is immediately taxed from 2% to 10%. Besides the probate, large fees are demanded for burying him in the chancel, his virtues are handed down to posterity on taxed marble; and he is then gathered to his fathers — to be taxed no more".

The taxes brought hardship to everybody, and the peasantry aided the bodies of men who rode in hundreds and were usually well mounted and armed to bring inland the contraband which the enterprising sea smugglers had brought to the shore.

These men were usually labourers, fishermen and the small traders, who became free traders as a spare time occupation for an extra source of income.

The seamen smugglers who sailed with the Captain were usually drawn from the local fishermen.

The land smugglers who helped the Lander were generally divided into two classes.

As late as 1833, these were the 'Riders', 'Carriers' or 'Bearers', whose earnings were 5/- and upwards each night; and the 'Batmen', who took their names from the 'Bat' or club which they used. 'The Batmen', usually disguised with black faces and using firearms, thought themselves superior, and protected the rest of the men. They earned 20/- or more a night. More often than not they received parish relief also!

The men were allowed a 'dollup' of tea (that is 40 lbs. weight worth about 25/- c. 1748), and their meals were paid for. They usually made one journey a week, but sometimes two or three.

The profits from a successful run were such that if they could safely land one cargo in three they were amply rewarded, and their profits allowed for the capture of their boat.

Very fine Cognac from Roscoff, Cherbourg, Dieppe and other French ports and the Channel Islands was landed on the shore of Christchurch and Bourne Heath. The 'tubs', each holding four gallons of Cognac, cost £1 in France and could be sold in England for £4. The liquor was 70° above proof, but cargoes as much as 180° above proof were brought over.

An ordinary lugger used for this purpose, and built on racing lines, could hold 80 tubs hidden in a false bottom or false keel. So fast were these luggers that a naval commander reported in 1815 that to order a revenue cutter to chase them was "like sending a cow after a hare".

If the smugglers were hard pressed by the revenue cutters they would sink their cargo — the tubs being roped together and weighted with sinking stones and grappled for later when the coast was clear. If this operation were delayed, and certain liquors remained under salt water too long, the cargo was rightly called stinkibus — undoubtedly High Spirits!

Many valuable cargoes were saved by being sunk, but these deep sea spirits could not rest until they had been landed on some deserted beach or in some quiet harbour, there to be quickly gathered into covered waggons by the Lander and his men, who slung the surplus tubs fore and aft on their strong bodies. Then they continued their restless journey to a hiding place until they could be quietly marketed inland. The hiding place might be deep in the sand, under flagstones, in the pulpit and tombs of churches, in a cellar or down a well. If a keg in a well cracked, someone might start the day with a miraculous glow after his early morning tea.

To keep down this illicit trading, the Government passed the Smugglers Act in 1736. This authorised the death penalty for smugglers dangerously wounding an Excise officer or hindering him in the execution of his duty. They were liable to punishments of five years' transportation or a month's hard labour for resisting officers. Authorised awards were given to informers by way of free pardons and money.

Although the majority of the local people were in league with the smugglers, there were still many who eagerly sought to 'string up' their sinful neighbours.

In 1752 Horace Walpole observed "It is shocking to think what a shambles this country is grown! Seventeen were executed this morning."

2

Smuggling Ways

THE smuggler was a practical man, generally speaking, and many and ingenious were his ways of concealing and disposing of his goods.

The winter was a favourite time of the year for the free traders, and the best characteristics of the British seamen were displayed when they undertook the terrible hardships and risks which accompanied a run.

Apart from the weather, the hazards to be overcome were the presence of the Revenue Cutters afloat, and the coast-guard and mounted guard on shore.

Some of the most successful smugglers had already served in the coastguard and so knew the duties and routine of the coastguard service. On the other hand many smugglers joined the ranks of the coastguard.

The direct landing of contraband at the end of a run was preferred, but if the risks were too great, then the goods, if spirits, would be sunk, and markers of cork or feathers would be left, and then the contraband would be grappled for later when the coast was clear.

If a gale threatened the safety of the boat, it was customary for the smugglers to 'lighten ship' by slipping out all the tubs on a long rope to which sinking stones had been attached and to ride with them until the weather conditions were better.

A 'forced run' was one carried out when a large and valuable contraband was at stake. In this case a 'fighting gang' protected the tub carriers with 'bats' (long ash bludgeons), and firearms. Serious fights took place between the free-traders and preventive men.

Free-trading became big business, and during the late 18th and early 19th centuries a vast amount of capital was invested in the smuggling transactions, often in small amounts by the local traders, doctors, parsons or any other interested parties.

The venturers or patrons employed 'freighters'. These were men who collected the money from their patrons and then proceeded to charter a vessel and buy the contraband from a foreign port. They usually returned with the vessel.

Before embarking, the freighter and the lander arranged details of the time and place of the landing. There were alternative arrangements in case of trouble with the Preventive Service.

Communications between the freighter and landing party were somewhat hazardous. It needed good judgement on the Lander's part to time the vessel's arrival off the shore, for the tide and wind varied, and the landing would generally take place on a moonless night.

When the cargo was due the shore party watched all the approaches to the landing place and immediately set off a warning to the boat at sea in case of alarm.

The signals were usually a fire lighted on a prominent headland — such as Hengistbury Head, Bournemouth, or what is now Steamer Point, Highcliffe in Hampshire—or a 'flink' with a flint and steel which could be spotted quite easily by the practised eye on a dark night—even a mile from the shore—and perhaps a flash from a dark lantern, or spout lantern, which was so constructed as to throw a bright light sea-ward whilst concealing the rays from observers on either side.

The pilot-smuggler who guided the vessel in with cat-like acuteness of vision to the appointed spot was known as a 'Spotsman'.

These men were usually employed when the master of the vessel was a stranger to the coasts, and often the freighter acted as the spotsman.

When the coast was clear the lugger anchored at a convenient distance from the shore. The sinking stones were cut loose from the line to which the tubs were fastened. The end of the line was made fast to a punt or small ship's boat and the tubs were towed to the beach. The tub-carriers waded out to receive the cargo, which was floated or 'rafted' ashore.

Horses and carts, commandeered from the local farmers, were ready in waiting for the contraband. Double Dykes, on Hengistbury Head, formed an ideal base for the Lander and his men.

Richard Warner (a pupil at Christchurch Grammar School between 1776 and 1780) writes in his *Literary Recollections*,

> "The shore of the noble promontory, Hengistbury Head, at the southern extremity of the united Avon and Stour rivers, was a spot frequently chosen as a landing place for the con-

traband goods. Of this grand feature of the coast, our elevated school-room (St. Michael's Loft, Christchurch Priory), which runs over the chancel of the church, commanded a perfect view; and with the assistance of a tolerable glass (telescope) enabled us to distinguish every moving object on the declivity of Hengistbury Head. I have myself, more than once, seen a procession of twenty or thirty waggons loaded with kegs of spirits; an armed man sitting at the front and tail of each; and surrounded by a troop of two or three hundred horsemen, everyone carrying on his enormous saddle from two to four tubs of spirits; winding deliberately and with the most picturesque and imposing effect, along the skirts of Hengistbury Head, on their way towards the wild country to the northwest of Christchurch, the point of their separation.

The revenue troop, who had always intelligence of the run, were, it is true, present on the occasion, but with no other views and intentions, than those of perfect peace. A flood of homely jokes was poured upon them by the passing ruffians; but, these were always accompanied by a present of kegs, greater or less, according to the quantity of smuggled goods; a voluntary toll received as it was conferred, in perfect good humour, and with mutual satisfaction."

Once the goods were landed they were removed as speedily as possible to pre-arranged destinations. Breweries, farms, manor houses, churches, tombs, wells and under flagstones were all used as hiding places.

In one case a farmer at Wick, or 'Week' as it used to be called, Bournemouth, woke up one morning to find that one of his hayricks had been moved from one place to another. A hard pressed lander and his men had re-built the rick round a load of tubs of brandy!

Although the methods used by the free-traders to smuggle contraband to our shores were somewhat naïve according to our present day ideas, they were very successful.

Silk, cloth and laces found a ready market. To hide these, whole hams were hollowed out and the materials were inserted, the outer skin being then sewn up and rolled in sawdust.

Between 1712 and 1835 there was a duty on soap, and no doubt many a little boy had a splendid excuse for not washing behind his ears, even though smuggled soap may have been cheap.

Although oppressed by the American and Napoleonic wars, the ladies of fashion were eager to know the latest modes and coiffures of the day. Little dolls dressed in the latest style were smuggled in from France so that the ladies of fashion could be satisfied.

Clarissa (c. 1760), a doll in the Red House Museum, Christchurch, Hampshire, was most likely a 'fashion doll', and may have had many an adventure to tell us if she could only speak. †

Pearls, cards and gloves were valuable cargo. Since the duty on French gloves was only payable on pairs, sometimes the left hand gloves were sent to London and right hand gloves were sent to Folkestone. When the goods were offered for sale very cheaply, the importer bought and paired the gloves and made a handsome profit. Whether the left hand ever knew where the right one was, no one knows.

Tea cases were fitted between the vessel's timbers and were made to resemble the floors of the ship.

18 lbs. of tea could be hidden under the cape or petticoat trouser worn by the fishermen and pilots of the vessels.

Cotton bags made into the shape of the crown of a hat, a

† Clarissa is now held in the Winchester Museum, Hampshire.

cotton waistcoat, and a cotton bustle and thigh pieces carried in all 30 lbs. of tea.

Tobacco, another taxed commodity, was valuable contraband. Made into ropes of two strands, it was coiled with the real rope in the lugger, and was even put into a special compartment in casks of imported bones which were used for manufacturing glue.

The wooden fenders slung over the sides of a ship were hollowed out and filled with tobacco.

There were other ways of bringing in extra tobacco without actual smuggling. As tobacco readily absorbs moisture from the air, it increases in weight in damp localities. One manufacturer avoided paying too much duty on his cargo by establishing a series of drying rooms on one of the Channel Islands. This room was heated to 90° and he despatched large quantities of leaf tobacco to the depot.

After it had dried out the tobacco was tightly packed into barrels and then imported to England. He paid the duty on the dried tobacco, thus tobacco weighing 100 lbs. could, by drying, be reduced to 60 lbs.

It was then taken to a factory, unpacked, and exposed to the air, and regained its original weight. A handsome profit was made by the manufacturer. Later, a law was passed imposing duty on tobacco "according to the quantity of moisture contained therein". Since the rate was higher if the tobacco was dried, then there was no point in the tobacco being dry.

Spirits, both brandy and gin, had intriguing journeys into our ports.

Brandy was chiefly imported from France. Excellent cognac was shipped from Roscoff. Gin, popular with the troops who had taken part in the Dutch wars, was imported from the Low Countries. Flushing exported gin chiefly to the East Coast.

Brandy or gin tubs, roped singly or in pairs and anchored with sinking stones, could be cut off easily and left with markers if Revenue Cutters were in sight.

Tubs of spirits were packed into the hollowed keels of boats, hidden under false bottoms, or fitted into rafts or punts which were floated on a flood tide to persons waiting on the shore.

In his book on Boldre, in the New Forest, Mr. Frank Perkins tells about smugglers at Pitts Deep, Boldre, Hampshire.

> "The kegs of spirits, roped together, were sunk and marked with a float, about one quarter of a mile from the shore, in the Pitts Deep stream, at a spot known as Brandy Hole. The kegs were floated ashore by punts, as by this way it was easier to sink them if a coastguard arrived.
>
> The kegs were carried from the shore by a gang of local men to carts which were waiting a short distance away, but if dangerous for the carts to load up, the kegs were easily slung across the shoulders, generally one in front and two behind. The pay was 2/6d. per keg. To assist the coastguards, a mounted man called a riding officer, lived in a cottage near Pylewell Home Farm. The smugglers did not mind this man as he could be easily watched."

It is said that before 1858 the tide came up to Haywood Mill and possibly as far as Brockenhurst.

At high tide in the marsh Boldre Bridge was reached by

ships which anchored there. There was also a deep channel of some kind which came along the marsh from Lymington, all very convenient to the smugglers.

Not only were women useful to the smugglers as signallers and carriers of messages from members of the gang to each other, but they actually brought goods in from the shore for them.

The voluminous skirt was a particularly useful fashion, for the women wound yards of silk and lace round their bodies and reached home as a rule quite peacefully with their contraband.

There have been cases, however, when women have, on inspection, been found to have had their petticoats puffed out by bladders filled with spirits.

A report from a Hampshire Chronicle of March 25th 1799 stated that,

> "A woman of the name of Maclane, residing at Gosport, accustomed to supply the crew of *Queen Charlotte* with slops went out in a wherry to Spithead, when a sudden squall coming on, the boat sank; the watermen were drowned, but the life of the woman was providentially saved, by being buoyed up with a quantity of bladders, which had been secreted round her for the purpose of smuggling liquor into the ship, until she was picked up by the boat of a transport lying near."

A case of being buoyed up by good spirits no doubt!

Customs records show that in 1764 ships of the East India Company smuggled tea into this country estimated at seven million pounds annually.

To the east of Aden the whole of Britain's commercial

products were under the control of the East India Company, and this monopoly lasted until 1833.

An East Indiaman, the *Thames,* loaded with silks and other fine materials, arrived off the Scilly Isles. A pilot boat in which were six or seven men came alongside.

These men went aboard the *Thames* and hurried to the mate's cabin, where they inspected the rich silks and other materials displayed there.

They quickly wound the materials round their bodies, and a further supply was hastily handed down in packing cases to the waiting boat. The pilot and his men then returned to the islands.

An informer gave the game away to the Customs and the chief officer of the *Thames* was heavily fined.

Not only were the free traders responsible for bringing in goods for the comfort of mankind, but also people themselves proved to be valuable contraband.

In the first few years of the French Revolution and during the Reign of Terror, the Christchurch Smugglers helped the Aristocrats to escape from 'Madame Guillotine' to the safety of England. Beech House, Bransgore, was said to have been a rendezvous for the fugitives from France. A document in Romsey Abbey states that three refugee regiments had been formed from the noble blood of France.

The document, written in French, is addressed to M. le Juge de Paix, calling his attention to the unhappy position of certain French Royalists who were emigrés in Romsey, and testifying to the hardships suffered by men and officers who served with the Royal and Christian Army in the attack against the French Republicans at Quiberon on the 16th July 1795, an ill-starred expedition led by Marquis de St. Suzanne from which only one or two escaped massacre and imprisonment.

Signed by the Marquis du Dresnay, the Marquis de St. Suzanne, Major Count de la Monneraye, and Quarter Master Le Grand Harscouet de St. Georges, the document concludes with this passage:

> "In testimony where-of we have drawn up this report on the evidence of M. le Grand and Harscouet de St. Georges, officers of our regiment, eye witnesses, who escaped in a miraculous way from all those massacres and who attested with us."

A French priest, John Franke Poisson, who was undoubtedly an emigré from the Parish of St. Eny, Diocese Contance, escaped to England and was buried at Romsey Abbey on September 23rd, 1796. The deaths of many more French emigrés are listed in "Old Times Revisited" by E. King. One being Joseph Marie de la Moussaye, Major of the Corps of Loyal Emigrants, buried in 1813 in Lymington Churchyard.

The Duc de Gramont, Captain of the Gard du Corps of Louis XVI was attacked at Versailles in 1792, and he escaped to England. It is supposed that his daughter was smuggled to the Duchess of Devonshire's care. She married the Earl of Tankerville and their daughter, Corisande, became the Countess of Malmesbury. Her tomb is in the Priory Church, Christchurch.

Those with other particular problems found the smugglers helpful too.

The Hon. Mrs. Stuart Wortley wrote,

"Pamela (was) indubitably the daughter of Madame de Genlis and Philippe Egalité, Duc d'Orléans.
Her birth was kept secret, and the babe was smuggled out of France and taken to England and there placed with a woman called Syms living at Christchurch. When six years old Madame de Genlis 'found' her and brought her back to France to be educated with the children of the Orléans family. She married Lord Edward Fitzgerald."

It was difficult enough for the Preventive Service to cope with the illicit trade which prevailed in peacetime, but in war-time the smugglers were a great threat to the country's security, and with their luggers heavily armed, and possibly employed by the enemy, they harassed the already over-worked Revenue Cruisers.

Napoleon regarded the smugglers as his fifth column and used them as channels of communication for his spies. He also needed vast amounts of gold to continue his struggles and he employed English men to transport gold to his empty coffers via Holland.

A document of the Royal Courts of Guernsey stated that in 1800 many cargoes of gold amounting to between ten or twelve thousand English guineas each week reached France. For every guinea deposited in Napoleon's treasury the French Government paid between 25/- and 30/-.

The guineas were transported in

"boats of 40 ft. or more in length, on a breadth of 6½ and 7 feet, rowed by twenty four or thirty six men. They were called 'guinea boats' and their rate of rowing in a calm sea was from 7 to 9 miles an hour, so that it was extremely difficult to take them."

Deal and Folkestone were notorious for their connection with 'guinea smuggling'.

As Napoleon said, "They (the English) have the courage and ability to do anything for money . . . "

Since this book was first published some information about smuggling in the 16th century has been received from Mrs. B. Peters of Christchurch.

After the Reformation, and particularly during the reign of Elizabeth I, there was considerable traffic in human contraband and religious books.

When measures were taken to suppress the Roman Catholic faith, the Christchurch area was a particularly strong pocket of resistance, and children were smuggled out of the country to be given a Roman Catholic education abroad. Whole families sometimes departed to escape the religious persecution of those days, and many young men left secretly to travel to the seminaries in France and Belgium, returning, in disguise, after ordination as priests, to minister to the religious needs of those who, despite cruel penalties, had remained true to the Faith of their fathers. These people, known as recusants, refused to attend the service of Common Prayer in the Church of England that was made compulsory for all under the Act of Uniformity (1 Eliz. C2 1559), and refused to acknowledge the Queen as Supreme Head of the Church of England (Act of Supremacy 29th April, 1559).

Hampshire was a 'key' recusant county, and in May, 1559, it was said that the number of Roman Catholics in Hampshire 'frightened the Queen and Council'.

No books could be printed in England without episcopal licence, but many religious books were produced in Lovain and Antwerp. Between 1564 and 1568 no less than 20,000 of these 'naughty' books were known to have been smuggled into England. Who knows what the complete total must have been!

3

The Preventive Service

DURING the latter part of the 18th century and early 19th century the work of the Preventive Service was hampered because the Government employed totally inadequate forces to combat the smuggler. It was, however, difficult for the Government to supply sufficient forces for this service, especially during the Revolutionary Napoleonic Wars.

The Christchurch Barracks were built in 1795 when smuggling was at its peak, and frequently the Dragoons supported the Preventive men on land, yet their combined forces were often completely routed in the pitched battles which took place with the free traders.

The advent of the military forces was of tremendous help, for not only did they guard the coasts against the enemy, but also assisted the local Preventive men with their work, although it would seem that relations between the civilians and the forces were hampered by some jealousy and lack of co-operation at times!

The Informers, who were hated generally by both sides, were of great use to the Preventive Service, and were paid for their help. They lived a precarious existence because they always ran the risk of being maltreated by the smugglers.

At sea, the Revenue Service had their difficulties, and to catch a fast lugger with their 'guard-ships — generally of the frigate type' was, at times, almost impossible.

"Notwithstanding our shooting", reported a Naval Officer, "the smugglers would pull in the wind's eye and escape with the greatest of ease."

For customs and preventive purposes, Southampton was the head or Mother Port. The Hampshire Repository for 1798 states that Christchurch and Lymington were 'creeks'.

> "A creek, in the language of the customs, is a place included within the limits either of a head or member port, as set out by the commissioners of the court of exchequer, and at which officers competent to transact the coast business are stationed by order of the board of customs. The creek is in like manner with the member port subject to the authority of the patent officers."

Lymington was the only creek in Hampshire where "not only coal duties, but all other coast duties were received, without the merchant being under the necessity of applying to the head or member port, there being a collector, comptroller and a coast waiter stationed there for that purpose."

The Establishment at Southampton, the head or Mother port, consisted of the Principal Officers who were a collector, comptroller, landing surveyor, four landing waiters and a searcher, assisted by a tide surveyor, 16 boatmen and tide-waiters (resident at port).

Also, for the convenience of the coasting trade, apart from

the officers stationed at Lymington, was a coast waiter, whose duty was to supervise the loading and discharging of coasting vessels at the following places: —

'Bewley', Keyhaven, Redbridge, Christchurch, Heath Leap and Hamble.

He also performed additional duty as a riding officer, and with four others, "expressly called riding officers, formed a guard from Southampton to Christchurch being the whole district of the port of Southampton."

As a further guard a cutter was established, and this was of about 100 tons with a commander and 30 men. A Mr. Williams, mate of the *Batt* cutter standing off Christchurch Bay, is mentioned in the journals of a Customs and Excise Officer, Abraham Pike of Christchurch. There were also two row boats with six men in each, and a superior officer over them, stationed at Christchurch and Lymington.

DEPUTED OFFICERS AT CHRISTCHURCH 1804: —

The Supervisor of Customs and Coast Waiter — Abraham Pike.
Four Riding Officers.
Sitter of the boat — John Williams.
Six boatmen.

These men were not very well paid; for example, a Riding Officer responsible for a very wide patrol area was paid a salary of £25 per annum with an allowance for keeping a horse — which he had to supply himself. These figures were disclosed in a letter to London dated May 23rd, 1775, when a report stated that John Florence, Riding Officer for Lytchett Bay to Studland Bay, was unable to perform his duties through illness.

Further information from the Admiralty states that

> "Christchurch was the headquarters of a 'district' in the preventive service, with responsibility for the Coast from Calshot Castle to Handfast Point. Preventive stations were situated at Lepe, Hurst Castle, Christchurch, Bourne Chine and Branksea Island. The whole district being under the command of a retired lieutenant of the Royal Navy."

Branksea Island, now Brownsea, situated at the narrow entrance to Poole Harbour, was an ideal station for the men of the Customs, because they could keep a close watch on all shipping entering or leaving the harbour.

During the winter of 1821 Captain Marryat, R.N. in his brig *Rosario* spent his time with the Revenue Cutters cruising between Portsmouth and Start Point, his chief patrol areas being Weymouth, Beer and Dartmouth.

Marryat disclosed his feelings about the Preventive service in a letter to the First Lord of the Admiralty;

> "I now proceed to state the measures at present resorted to by the Revenue Cruizers employed in the prevention of the Contraband trade. These vessels are more at anchor than at sea, and when under weigh are seldom out of sight of the English Coast."

The Preventive Service was, in his eyes, "inefficient and badly organised".

Oliver Warner in his book on Captain Marryat stated:

> "Although he (Marryat) and his kind received blood money for every smuggler captured, together with shares in the seizures made, he perceived that only drastic remedies would be any real use. 'Seize the vessels', he urged, 'saw them up; draft the crews into the navy'."

For the most part men of the Preventive Service were loyal, able and conscientious in their work. They had an unenviable task, and indeed sometimes succumbed to bribery. Christchurch was fortunate in having in its district such reliable excisemen as Mr. Abraham Pike, Mr. Richard Newman and Mr. John North.

Pitt the younger, who became Prime Minister in 1783, began to make it unprofitable for the smugglers to bring in their contraband. For instance, in 1784 he reduced the duty on tea from about 120% to 12%, making the brands of the cheapest tea available at about 3/6d. per pound.

Although Pitt lowered the duties and reduced the number of goods liable to Excise, it was not until after the Battle of Waterloo in 1815 that the large scale free-trading industry finally began to dwindle. There were then more men available to man the coasts, and gradually Coastguards replaced the Riding Officers and Revenue Cutters.

The Coastguard Officers and their men were housed at strategic places on the coast.

Although the Haven House at Mudeford, Christchurch, had been commandeered as a Preventive Station in 1823 and was in use as such as late as 1857, another parcel of land approximately two acres in extent was purchased by the Crown from the vendor G. Belbin, by conveyance dated the 14th August, 1861.

Upon this land the Crown erected in 1861/2:

a) An Officer's House, consisting of five bedrooms, two sitting rooms, kitchen, scullery and pantry. This is now called the Chart House.

b) Ten Coastguard Cottages, each containing three bedrooms, one living room and a scullery. These are still called Coastguard Cottages today.

c) A Boathouse and Store with Watch Room and Office.

In 1869, a site at Mudeford for a boathouse was granted by Lady Waterford rent free, upon which the Crown erected a portable boathouse.

All these buildings were close to or overlooked the harbour. and no ship could slip through the Avon run without being spotted by the coastguard.

The Preventive Service had to contend with increasing criticism, although they did seize a remarkable amount of contraband.

The following account, printed by the House of Commons, showed these dutiable items collected by the Coastguard or Preventive Water Guard, Riding Officers and Revenue Cruisers and Ships of war between 1822 and 1825: —

Tobacco	902,684¼ lbs.
Snuff	3,000 lbs.
Brandy	135,000 gallons
Rum	253 gallons
Gin	227,000 gallons
Whisky	10,500 gallons
Tea	19,000 lbs.
Silk	42,000 yds.
India handkerchiefs	2,100 pieces
Leghorn hats	23
Cards	3,600 packs
Timber	10,000 pieces
Stills	75

The Revenue Coastguard established in 1831 was transferred from the Board of Customs to the control of the Admiralty in 1856. This naval force was officially known as the 'First Naval Reserve'.

The Coastguard thus became in a sense a naval man ashore.

Though the Coastguard were not now controlled by the Customs and Excise, they were there to help to discourage further smuggling.

The measures taken by the Government, and the coming of steam in place of sail together with the establishment of long distance communications combined to make the trade uncertain for any venturer and so smuggling on a grand scale died out.

There are, of course, still cases of smuggling, but attempts to evade the payment of duty on valuable goods are not now so simple or naïve as they were in the 18th and early 19th centuries. So long as prices are artificially increased by the imposition of dues and duties no doubt there will be those who will exercise ingenuity and imagination to circumvent those dues and duties, no matter what the risks may be.

4

Officers of Customs & Excise

THE Riding Officers of Excise for Christchurch, Hampshire, were based at No. 10 Bridge Street, Christchurch, which was the Headquarters of Excise. †

As the Supervisor of Excise, one of the officers, Abraham Pike, lived a hazardous and hard life. His journal of 1803-1804 shows absolute devotion to duty against difficult odds. He recorded faithfully his long daily journeys in the tracking of smugglers. His duties took him out during the night, too, and after long and fruitless searches he must have been disheartened time and again. There were, however occasions when his success compensated him for his disappointments.

One of his entries in his journal reads:

"October 4 1804 Collected my officers Journals for the Past Month afterwards set out with Mr Bacon to the West Coast on Discoveries. In the Heath we saw a fire lighted up at Bourn we immediately went to the spot by the time we got there the fire was out the smugglers began flashing and striking of light as appeared to us by flint and steel all Night in Diferent parts of the heath and in the Cliffs we attended the Coast all Night and prevented them from landing the Night being so very dark we saw no person that was on the coast During the Night on my Return Informed Mr Williams mate of the Batt Cutter of the above proceedings afterward Mr Williams called to inform me the smugglers' had worked at the East. Set out with Mr Bacon and a Party Examind

† Although the Riding Officer's Diary for 1803-04 was found in the loft of this present building, it appears that it was not the Office of Customs and Excise. The present house was rebuilt circa 1863 on the site of a thatched house, owned by Abraham [Abram] Pike, which had burnt down. Mrs. G. Dixon, Abram Pike's great grand-daughter, states that he occupied one of a group of houses under the shadow of the castle in Christchurch, near to the old Court House. It was probably the house which is now a shop, next to the perfumery.

the crofs roads through the Forest found the smugglers was gone towards Minway At Minway met Mr Butler sitter of the Boat at Lymington and his Boat Crew who (m) informed us the smugglers had been flashing a(t) Beacon I met Mr. How and Mr Prichard and informed them the smugglers was looking out at Minway the(y) informed me the smugglers had worked the preceding Night between Beacon to Minway attended the Coast all Night and prevented them from landing"

If any contraband was seized it was usually impounded in the King's Custom House, situated on Poole Quay.

The Establishment Books listing all the Riding Officers in Southampton, Cowes and Poole Collection for the years 1782 and 1805 state the following:

Customs 62/2 Collector Southampton to Board
10th October 1823

Hon. Sirs,

We beg to apprize your Honble Board that Mr. Abraham Pike who has for many years been superannuated from the Customs (having been a Supervisor of Riding Officers) died yesterday at Xchurch within this Port.

We are etc.
S.L.F.

There is a tomb in Christchurch Priory Churchyard on which is the inscription:

'Sacred to the memory of Abraham Pike who departed this life Oct. 17th 1823 Aged 72 years . . .'

It is possible that this could be the same man.

Mr. Richard Newman was another hardworking man. He was the Riding Officer of Excise for Christchurch in 1799.

A story attributed to him gives some idea of the patience needed by such a man in the course of his duties.

Generally speaking the free-traders preferred to land their cargoes on moonless nights, but occasionally they changed their tactics. In an all-out attempt to catch the smugglers Mr. Richard Newman, with his brother officers, spent several fruitless nights lying in shallow 'graves' dug along the coast at intervals from Chewton Bunny to Hengistbury Head. Camouflaged with seaweed, covered with sand and heavily armed, they surveyed the coastline of the bay.

The ruse did prove successful, for a landing was made, and, as the lander was late, the contraband was left on the shore, unguarded.

To their great astonishment the tardy land smugglers found themselves surrounded by excisemen who, at a signal from Newman, emerged from the sands. Thoroughly startled, they fled from the shore leaving their goods behind them.

On the following day the Customs men saw that the confiscated contraband was put into waggons. These were drawn by horses under the care of their owners who were reasonably reliable men. Without a Military or Excise escort the convoy set off for the Custom House at Poole.

As it was a very hot day the waggoners rested their horses before they attempted the long pull up Poole Hill. Feeling thirsty, the men were tempted to drink some of the free-traders' brandy. Thereupon they fell asleep. The horses, restless in their harness and the heat, turned round and took their waggons back to their stables at Christchurch.

The extraordinary thing about this was that no one had attempted to interfere with them on their return journey and the brandy was still safe in the waggons.

Mr. John North (1780-1860) was a conscientious and

reliable exciseman. He was the great-grandfather of Mr. Donovan Lane of Orchard Close, Stour Road, Christchurch.

According to extracts taken from the Excise Board's Minutes, Mr. John North was, in 1808, a supernumerary in the Isle of Wight Collection, and in 1815 he was in the Newport Division. At intervals he was transferred to Collections in Bristol, Sarum and Surrey. He was in the Christchurch Division from 1842 to 1848.

Mr. North finally retired owing to ill health in 1850. He was buried in Christchurch Cemetery.

The famous poet from Scotland, Robert Burns, became an Exciseman, although during the early part of his life he was not averse to doing a little smuggling himself. In 1778 he wrote:

> "I spent my nineteenth summer on a smuggling coast, a good distance from home. The contraband trade was at that time very successful and it sometimes happened to me to fall in with those who carried it on."

Later in life, as an Inspector of Liquor Customs during the year 1792, he carried out a difficult raid on a smuggling lugger in Solway Firth.

Since the dragoons, excise officers and his party were not able to get to the boat, Burns entered the water, braved the dangerous quicksand — and the free-traders, boarded the vessel and captured the crew. He then took the ship to Dumfries to be sold.

Robert Burns was an Excise gauger well known to the smugglers, and Mr. Neville Williams says of him, "He was not a bustling fellow as far as his duty was concerned, nor did he love to put himself forward in adventures which he knew would bring distress to many."

These brave Officers of His Majesty's Customs and Excise had an unenviable job to do, and the majority were well respected for their diligence, but, whenever there was a chance, the smugglers liked to get the better of them.

One Scottish story is of some excisemen who returned to an inn for the night after capturing a whisky keg. Overjoyed by their success they danced round the keg which they had left on the floor in the centre of their room.

Sitting on the keg was one of their number who felt sure it would be safe for the night.

It certainly was there in the morning, but alas, it was empty! During the night someone in the inn who knew the exact position of the keg had bored a hole through the ceiling of the room below and into the keg . . . ! !

"Ye men of wit and wealth, why all this sneering
'Gainst poor Excisemen? Give the cause a hearing.
What are your landlord's rent rolls — taxing ledgers:
What Premiers — what; — even monarch's mighty gaugers:
Nay, what are priests, those seeming godly wise men?
What are they, pray, but spiritual Excisemen?"

Robert Burns: *circa* 1789

5

Christchurch Barracks

THE Bailey Bridge, which was so fimiliar to all the allied armies during the second world war, and without which, some say, the war would not have been won, had its origins in the then War Ministry Experimental Establishment in Barrack Road, Christchurch. The name Barrack Road itself suggests the more humble beginnings of this famous establishment.

The guard room, which still stands close to the main road, was a part of the original Christchurch Barracks, and is now preserved as a building of historic interest.

The first Barracks, according to the Fourth Report of the Commissioners of Military Enquiry, were ordered to be built by Major General Oliver de Lancey, Barrack Master General. to accommodate three troops of cavalry.

The work was done by John Pelgram, or Pilgrim, on land bought for the purpose, and completed in 1795.

The 20th Dragoons were stationed there.

The threat of invasion of our coasts by the French moved the Government to strengthen its forces by bringing more cavalry into this area. Another factor which could have added to the urgency for military help was the need for the suppression of smuggling in the area.

A letter sent in 1770 by Mr. Richard Huges, of Wick near Christchurch, to the military authorities showed concern for the widespread illicit trading: —

> "I beg to inform you that there are two bays or arms of the sea on each side of Christchurch in Hampshire that are continually frequented by a most dangerous band of smugglers, who appear to hold all the revenue laws in open defiance. I venture to recommend that a troop of dragoons should be sent to Christchurch. At this very moment the smuggling cutter is lying in Christchurch Bay flying His Majesty's colours."

In 1812 an extension to the Barracks was completed to accommodate an extra troop of horse artillery, at a cost of £7,365. Further Army Estimates for 1875-6 and 1876-7 show that at this time the Barracks were again enlarged at a cost of £3,500.

There was not always perfect accord between the Dragoons and the Riding Officers of Customs and Excise. The soldiers resented being under the command of the Riding Officer, who was a civilian, and whose official description until 1822 was "a man of authority with soldiers under him". Soldiers traditionally dislike the role of policemen, and there may well have been among the dragoons some from local families, whose own brothers were smugglers. Certainly, as with the majority of the local inhabitants, their sympathies tended to lie with the smugglers rather than with the civilian officers.

In spite of friction, however, it was reported that in a single half-year after the Barracks were built, 5,400 gallons of spirit and 7,600 lbs. of tea were captured from the smugglers and brought into Southampton, and similar captures were made at other places along the coast.

Whether the soldiers liked it or not, they certainly played their part in putting down the smugglers.

A treasury Warrant (c. 1720) is on record, having been issued to a regiment for the sum of £200 required to renew boots and stockings worn out in the chasing of smugglers!

Guard Room, Christchurch Barracks

6

The Eight Bells

TUCKED away in a short narrow street leading to the Christchurch Priory Church is an enchanting shop standing under the old sign of *The Eight Bells*.

This shop was, for centuries before, an inn. During the eighteenth and early nineteenth centuries it must have seen its hey-day, at a time when its two portly publicans were members of the Christchurch corporation.

They were, according to Warner,

> "A father and son, by the name of Holloway, who at the sign of *The Eight Bells* vended, among other strong drinks, that justly esteemed concoction of malt and hops, then highly celebrated under the name of Ringwood Beer".

Inside the gay shop the low oak-beamed ceilings and stone floors are a reminder of its past history. Here, now, opposite the door, must have been the bar with an oak settle by the fireplace, where the old fishermen talked of brandy kegs and baccy and wondered whether the youngsters would have a good 'catch' that night —

" 'Tes dark, see, and no moon about".

Perhaps there'd be more strong brandy about tomorrow.

That's a nice secluded corner at the back, under the second beam — just the place for the Churchwardens of the Priory who might have slipped away during the sermon to fortify themselves with a quiet smoke and drink.

Could the cupboard at the top of the narrow, winding oak stairs have hidden a hunted man? Gulliver perhaps? That Gentle Smuggler of Poole who often escaped so narrowly to some quiet corner of Hampshire.

Did he leave his wig in that little cupboard by the fireplace as he rested until all was quiet again?

In that little dressing room . . . Whose lovely face has gazed into the mirror and smiled, secretly thinking, perhaps, of the handsome Dragoon who had swaggered past the window to Church that day?

The beams and old walls know the secrets of the past. We can only imagine what happened. There is, however, a story about *The Eight Bells* which was found inscribed on a wooden plaque on the wall of the inn.

There was sudden panic in *The Eight Bells.* A tub of brandy stood boldly on the stone floor, and the Customs officers were just rounding the corner.

"Oh", said Holloway, "Here's a mess we're in, what'll we do with it?"

"Down the well," said one.

"There's no time".

"In the brewery at the back!"

"There's men out there", said Tom.

"Up the chimney, then".

"Fire's too hot", hissed Holloway.

"Get a bowl o' water", called Katie Preston, who'd been leaning at the door, "and bring up the tub and a chair by the fire, there. Now hurry, and I'll be back in a minute." She ran next door.

In a trice, Katie came back with a squealing, howling baby, just dragged from its feed, and spreading her skirts over the sides of the chair and the tub of brandy so hiding it completely, she rolled up her sleeves and plunged the baby into the bath of water. The door flew open, the officers entered and started to search the house.

"There," Katie cooed to the baby, who did not relish his unexpected bath, " 'tes a nice warm fire to bath a baby by and that's a fact, but —" and here she turned to the men, "would 'e mind shuttin' the door there, the poor mite'll catch his death o' cold. Are you wantin' to come over here?" The baby screamed, red in the face.

"No, no Madam," said the officer gallantly, "pray continue".

They went upstairs and carried on their search. As they returned they called to the host,

"We've found nothing here."

They opened the door and the baby screamed again.

"Good-day Madam, good-day," they called and went their way, followed by the outraged baby's screams, which drowned the chuckle from Tom, "My, you saved us that time Katie!"

7

Quartleys

THERE is a direct link between the memorial stone bearing the name Dr. Arthur Quartley in the south aisle of the Priory Church, Christchurch, Hampshire, and the Georgian house in Castle Street, Christchurch, now known as 'Quartleys'.

Dr. Quartley resided in this gracious house, which stands near the Town bridge. He enlarged the building whilst he lived there, and on the wall to the right of the coach entrance are his initials, 'A.Q.'.

A very popular medical practitioner, Dr. Quartley was also Mayor of Christchurch during 1833, and from 1836 to 1838. He died at the age of seventy-seven on January 4th, 1839.

The worthy doctor was certainly no smuggler, but, as with so many good citizens of Christchurch, he did not entirely escape contact with smugglers. The third Earl of Malmesbury, in his memoirs, tells of the following incident.

One dark night two men, their faces hidden in their greatcoats, hammered on Dr. Quartley's front door. When he opened a window, they urgently demanded that he should go to the aid of one of their comrades.

The doctor mounted his horse and accompanied them to the village of Bransgore, at the edge of the New Forest.

Here, lying on a cottage floor, severely wounded, was Tom, a young seaman smuggler. The doctor discovered that he had been shot in the back during a smuggling affray with Custom House officers.

Having extracted the ball, Dr. Quartley said that the wound was very serious, and the patient must be kept quiet.

"Well, Tom," said his friend, "will'st thee stay here and be hanged, or shall we tip thee in the cart?"

Tom went in the cart.

Some time later, Dr. Quartley found a keg of fine French brandy on the steps at the front of his house. Chalked on the keg were the words, "Left here for the Doctor's fee."

There is a tail-piece to this story.

Fifteen years later, Dr. Quartley was visiting a friend at Bisterne, and after dinner they went on the river. The boatman looked hard at the doctor, who said,

"My man, you look as though I should know you."

The boatman replied,

"Know me! Please your honour, I be he from whose back

you cut a slug fifteen years ago. Don't you mind on it?"

Certainly the seamen smugglers deserved to be described as hardy.

The remains of the "Naked Man" in the New Forest, near Wilverley Post

8

Mudeford

MUDEFORD, or Muddiford as it was called as late as 1881, was a favourite landing ground for the shadowy gentlemen of the night. This was then a quiet, sleepy village standing on the little stream of the Muddey or Mude which rises at Thorney Hill near Bransgore and flows south to enter Christchurch Harbour, near the Haven, though now it is ignominiously piped on its way through Mudeford.

It was easy for contraband to be landed on the sandy beach, but the free traders took considerable risks as they brought their goods inland, for their heavy waggons sank into the marshy land close to Stony Lane. If they were pursued they evaded capture by plunging into the reed beds, which were deep enough to shield them and their waggons and horses.

Mudeford, now growing more populated every year, once appealed especially to those who liked the quiet surroundings it then offered.

One of these people was the notorious and wealthy Baroness Feuchères, who subsequently became the duc de Bourbon's mistress or unofficial wife, and châtelaine of the Château de Chantilly. She escaped from France to Mudeford after being accused of the duc de Bourbon's murder. Helped by Beau Brummell and Lord Stuart de Rothesay she retired in 1831 to the solitude of Bure Homage, which had once been a farmhouse.

She passed her days in this quiet backwater strolling down Bure's leafy lanes or lazing on the shore watching the fishermen. No doubt she loved to hear the men talking, for she was a fisherman-smuggler's daughter from St. Helen's in the Isle of Wight.

Her name was then Sophy Dawes, the 'winkle picker', and she had now returned to the countryside where, many years before, as a beautiful young girl wearing breeches and boots, she had taken part one night in a smuggling run near the *Cat and Fiddle* Inn on the edge of the New Forest.

She must have remembered how she had been pursued and captured by a young naval officer, John Stuart, who thought she was a young smuggler. This chance encounter resulted in love at first sight for both of them.

Although far apart in birth and upbringing, this meeting led to Lieutenant John Stuart putting Sophy into his mother's care at Bure Homage whilst he was at sea.

Lady Stuart, the young officer's mother, was embarrassed at the turn of events, but her sister, Lady Buckingham, who was staying with her when Sophy was brought to the house, was so enchanted with the girl that she insisted on taking her back to London with her.

During her introduction to the gay London life she eventually met Beau Brummell, the famous Dandy of the Regency Period, at a card game. Another of her admirers was Lord Winchilsea, and it was as a member of his party that she came to meet the duc de Bourbon, who was a French refugee living in London at the time.

Sophy became the high stakes in a game of cards between Lord Winchilsea and the duke Lord Winchilsea lost his duke prize and, as the Hon. Mrs. Stuart Wortley wrote,

> "So Louis Henri, duc de Bourbon and Sophy Dawes embarked on a relationship that lasted for twenty years and made the fisherman's daughter châtelaine of one of the finest Châteaux in France.
>
> No mean pinnacle to reach for a Winkle Picker."

Bure Homage was demolished in 1957, and some of Mudeford's old character was removed with it.

Close to a pine plantation, and almost at the water's edge, the once solitary building known as Haven House with its stables and cottages on Haven Quay was, according to Miss F. G. Hamilton† of Mudeford, built about 1600. Parts of it may be of earlier date, for when a chimney was strengthened the workmen found some sixteenth century panelling. In Holland this kind of quaint seventeenth century building rising from the sides of canals has the same high pitched roof, dormer windows and steep gables as the Haven House, which may account for the name 'Dutch House' given to it in later years.

This house became an inn, and for many years was used as a boarding house for families of repute. It was then taken over by the government to house Preventive Officers, and in 1837 it housed one Lieutenant and ten coastguards.

† Miss Hamilton has since died.

Documents held by the Town Clerk of Christchurch relating to the Haven House refer to it as being "Commonly known or called by the name Avon or Haven House near Muddiford".

Together with its stables it stood on what used to be called Haven Quay, now Mudeford Quay. In 1845 buildings adjoining the house were built on the land where the stables once stood, and in 1856 a statutory Declaration refers to the "Haven House Inn Quay Preventive Station and two cottages", also to a John Bemister's boathouse, the stables, used as stores, and the land south west of Sandhills Plantation to the water's edge as all belonging to Sir George Henry Rose.

Another document of 1857 shows that all the buildings and premises were leased to Her Majesty's Customs as a Preventive Station. This was an ideal vantage point for the Preventive Officers, but, in 1860 the Crown ordered new premises to be built at Stanpit, Mudeford, to guard against smuggling.

About this time, the backbone and ribs of an old ship, thought to have been one of Nelson's flotilla which had been wrecked on the shore, lay on the beach at the Christchurch side of the Haven House.

Certainly the *Haven House Inn* has seen many changes and many exciting sea fights which took place at the entrance to the Harbour.

One such engagement was reported in the Salisbury and Winchester Journal of July 10th, 1784, after some smugglers from the Isle of Wight had landed their cargo at Mudeford:

"The *Orestes* sloop-of-war, Captain Ellis, Commander, lying in Cowes Roads, having advice that two smuggling vessels the property of Messrs. Leith and Parrott, would arrive at Christchurch Point at the mouth of the Avon, on Wednesday, laden with Tea and Brandy from Guernsey and Jersey, made a feint of steering to the westward, and arrived at Christchurch very unexpectedly on Thursday morning. The smugglers had already landed their cargoes and numbered about 300, most of them from the Town and neighbourhood."

When the *Orestes* arrived it was about 6 a.m. and she stood off shore whilst they manned two tenders. One of the boats was sent alongside the smugglers and demanded their surrender.

This summons was answered immediately by a discharge of small arms whereby the Captain of the tender was killed and many of the crew of the *Orestes* were injured.

Meanwhile a great many of the smugglers who were already on the shore were alarmed by the firing and they tried to rejoin their boats, undaunted by cannon and shot flying around them from the guns of the *Orestes*.

Pistols were fired from land and even from the windows of the Haven Inn to help the free traders. This action continued until nine in the evening when the smugglers were finally beaten, and many of the crew in the man o' war were killed in the battle.

On the following day the *Orestes* departed, taking with her the two smuggling vessels considered to be worth £4,000 and also their two long boats, which the smugglers had scuttled in the hope of preserving them. One of the smuggling luggers was quite new, and to be captured on her first trip was disastrous for her owners. The report from the journal continued:

> "The exertion and bravery of the crews were beyond example, and we cannot but lament that such resolution and courage were not employed in a better cause. The consternation of the townspeople and adjacent country was very great, and we are sorry to add that the whole of this part of the coast furnishes melancholy and very alarming proof to what height the evasion of Excise Laws is arrived."

Chain shot which was reputed to have been fired from the *Orestes,* hitting the *Haven Inn* chimney stack, was found under a hearthstone in what was once a kitchen of the inn.

It has been suggested that the smugglers were under the command of 'Slippery Rogers', nicknamed from his eel-like facility of escaping from his maritime pursuers.

He is traditionally known as the grandson of Henry Rogers, who was, in 1634, the Mayor of Christchurch. According to Mr. Russell Oakley, the Mayor was either the author or preserver of the puzzle epitaph in the Christchurch Priory graveyard:

> "We are not slain, but raysed,
> Raysed not to life, but to be buried twice by men of strife.
> What rest could living have, when dead had none.
> Agree amongst you now, we ten are one."
>
> *Hen. Rogers* 1641

One of 'Slippery Rogers' ' fine vessels was seen leaving Christchurch Quay by a young schoolboy at the Grammar School in St. Michael's Loft in the Priory and he always joined the crowd in cheering when she set out on her adventurous voyages. He described the scene:

"Her unequalled length and perfect symmetry of form; her thousands of square feet of white canvas courting the breeze, and swelling to the sun, her forty rowers sweeping the rippled surface of the river, with strong, well-measured stroke, and above all, her jolly crew of daring mariners: their careless mirth, their choral songs; and triumphant huzzas; mingled with parting salutes, and farewell wishes to their friends on shore; combined to produce an effect, that might well have moved the spirit of a much graver personage than an imaginative youth, who had seen only his eleventh or twelfth year."

The fate of this vessel formed a striking contrast to the gay scene as it left the harbour, for, on their homeward voyage Rogers and his crew never hesitated "to tempt the dangers of the deep", and always said they preferred a run "in thunder, lightning and in rain" because they then felt secure from the chase of the revenue cutters.

One night they left Havre during a terrible storm, and reaching Christchurch Bay, they approached at length the shore,

> "Where the associates of their lawless trade
> Kept watch; and to their fellows off at sea
> Gave the known signal:"

but the thunder of mountainous surf announced that landing was impossible. Heaven, in vain, held out its final warning. The fearless crew pushed madly for the beach; and in a few moments, their noble bark was bilged and shattered: and several of themselves, together with the cargo, were swallowed by the deep.

This was not only the fate of many smugglers, but Revenue Officers also lost their lives at sea in the course of their duties at much the same place, for one of the burial records at the Christchurch Priory states:

"Dec. 29, 1804 . . . Frances Tuckerbury, John Randall, Silas Carvel, Robert Fuzzard, the last four belonged to the Fox Revenue Lugger, in going over Christchurch Ledge in an open boat, the sail jibing and upset the boat, and were all drowned."

Another inn linked by tradition with the smugglers, which is conveniently sited on the edge of Stanpit Marsh, is the *Ship in Distress*. That this inn was kept by a certain Mother Sellars is certainly true,† and that she helped the smugglers to conceal their contraband and allowed the inn to be used as a rendezvous by them is credible. Her name has been immortalized by a water-way in the Stanpit Marsh leading to Stanpit and the inn being called Mother Sellars' Channel. The following story, which is quite readily told by the local people, is of Mother Sellars and a dashing Billy Coombs.

This handsome sea-faring Captain of a fast sailing vessel of about 100 tons and carrying 14 guns — sometime privateer and sometime smuggler — used frequently to drop in to smoke his pipe and drink ale with the widow known as the 'angel of the smugglers'. Mrs. Sellars fell in love with the Captain, and apparently the feeling was mutual, for he promised that when he returned from his next voyage he would marry her.

"How shall I know you'll be coming back to me?" she asked.

"I'll leave this package o' papers with you, me dear, they're important and I'll surely be back for them — and you."

He left the package, but Mrs. Sellars, consumed with curiosity, opened it, and from amongst the business papers fell a love letter from a girl at Hamble, where Coombs lived.

† Evidence from the Christchurch Poor Rate Book shows in 1780 a "widow Seller", and in 1797 a "Hannah Seller" living at the Haven House Inn. There is no hard evidence as yet to show that Mother Sellars (? Seller) lived at the Ship in Distress.

Mrs. Sellars read the letter, which said that the girl was longing for Billy's return when he would keep his promise and settle down and marry her!

Mrs. Sellars in a fury of jealousy, betrayed her lover to the Revenue Officers, telling them when he would return.

Accordingly H.M. brig *Osprey*, carrying 20 guns, was sent to Christchurch Bay, and as Coomb's lugger the *John and Sussannah* rounded Hengistbury Head she came under the guns of the man o' war.

The courageous Captain beat his crew to quarters and opened fire on the *Osprey* killing her Commander, Captain Allen.

The sound of the firing roused the whole of Christchurch, and everyone rushed down to see the spectacle. It has been said that one of the cannon balls even hit the Priory Church.

The fight continued fiercely for three hours, and after a desperate struggle the smuggling cutter was captured and taken to Cowes. The smugglers were 'pressed' on board a sloop of war, but Captain Coombs who had fired a gun, so it is said, after hauling down his colours, was tried and hanged from a gibbet at Stoney Point, Lepe. Some of his friends cut him down one night, and carried the body by cart to Hamble, where they awakened the parson and begged him to bury the Captain's remains in a Churchyard.

The Captain of the *Osprey* was buried at Cowes, where the circumstances of his death are recorded on a tombstone.

It is possible that there really was a Captain Billy Coombs, but the author W. H. G. Kingston, actually wrote a story called *Billy Coomb's Last Fight,* and whether the story was, in part, purely fiction or based wholly on fact, is not known.†

In a Hampshire Chronicle of 1798, there is mention of two breweries in the Parish of Christchurch. One was certainly at the rear of *The Eight Bells* in Christchurch, and there was, according to people living in Stanpit, a brewery close to the *Ship in Distress.* In fact, a Mr. William Stride was born in a cottage behind the brewery. A lantern*found on the site of the brewery when the old buildings were demolished, is in the Red House Museum at Christchurch. This could well have been of the type used by smugglers. The brewery was adjacent to the marshes, and it must have been ideal for the gentlemen to drop much of their cargo there before proceeding inland to the New Forest.

The Black House, which stands on the sand dunes at Gervis Point on Avon Beach, has an obscure history. It has been suggested that it was probably built either when the shipyard was started at Gervis Point, or by the Hengistbury Mining Company some time during the last century, although there is no proof of this.††

The Black House had a large section on the ground floor which was used for boat building. Some of the vessels built there could well have been the guinea boats, which were very fast sailing vessels used by the smugglers to take English gold over to Holland and subsequently to France, especially during the Napoleonic Wars. After the building of these boats was prohibited in England, they were then built in Calais.

Certainly there were ships built at the Haven, for on July 30th 1842, Mr. George Holloway launched a vessel of 200 tons, and in Lloyds register an entry states that "the *Enter-*

† In 1785 the High Court of the Admiralty gave the order for the execution of George Coombes, who was convicted of aiding and abetting in the murder of William Allen, late master of the sloop *Orestes.* One of the witnesses at the trial was Hannah Sellers. The Hampshire Chronicle in January 1786 reported that George Coombes left Newgate and was hanged at Execution Dock. His body was ordered by the Court of Admiralty "to be hung in chains near Christchurch Harbour, where the fact was committed".

* The lantern is now at the Winchester Museum, Hampshire.

†† The Black House was built circa 1840 by Mr. G. Holloway (q.v.) as a sail loft for his shipbuilding venture.

prise a brig of 253 tons was launched August 1848, dimensions 94 ft. long by 21 ft. 8 ins. by 15 ft."

A note of contract with builder of the latter boat reads: —

Christchurch March 22nd 1847.

"I hereby agree to give Mr. Ellwood Day the sum of Twenty six Shillings per ton (O.M.) that the vessel now on the stocks at Gervis Point may admeasure . . . be to finish and launch the said vessel according to Lloyd's rules: the said vessel being 256 tons or thereabouts.

Signed Geo. Holloway *Witness* C. R. Holloway."

The Black House was once inhabited by Mr. William Stride, a fisherman for over fifty years. His grandchildren live in Mudeford today. Many were the recollections Mr. Stride had of old smuggling days.

In the Black House were two secret cupboards. One was in the roof, but it was removed during some alterations to the building; the second is still believed to be in existence.

The Black House is now the only real building left on the Christchurch side of Hengistbury Head, but in the days when the ironstone quarry was worked there were several dwellings close to it.

It has been reported that during Mr. Stride's habitation of the Black House, the sea had broken through the sand dunes on at least three occasions.

This building formed a convenient hideout for the free traders. One story is told of some smugglers who were hiding in the Black House and could not be forced out by any means, so bonfires were lit all round the building and eventually they were forced out by the flames and smoke.

Mr. Wm. Stride could recall the last of the famous smugglers of Mudeford called Old Abe Coakes, who used to run the gauntlet of the Revenue Officers on Haven Quay.

Contraband, marked by floats, was dropped overboard from a vessel at the entrance to the Run, a narrow channel leading into Christchurch Harbour, and he would swim noiselessly up the Run with the tide towing casks of brandy fastened to a rope, as far as Smugglers' Ditch, Mother Sellar's Channel or, some say, even as far as Bergman's Mill on Christchurch Quay. This mill, supposed to have been owned by a Dutchman, was used for hiding contraband.

Another link with the smuggling past is what was formerly the charming *Moorings Hotel,* now divided into two private houses. Here the gentlemen of the night would meet and plan their ventures. The building was erected about the year 1700 by members of the Dutch Colony, and scratched on one of the original Dutch window panes is the date 1732, and the names

Van Doel, Van Tellir,
J. Verheiul.

Who were they, these Dutchmen, who gazed through the windows to see the beautiful harbour beyond so many years ago? What they were like, where they came from or when they left this part of the world no one seems to know, but certainly they have been here and left their mark for us to see in what was once called *The Dutchman's Inn.*

Other old inns with a smuggling history in the Christchurch district are *The Nelson, The Ship, The Dolphin* and *The George.* Whether the *King's Arms* ever entertained the smugglers is not known, but it could have been a quiet retreat for a squire or other wealthy venturers.

There are many tales of adventures by moonlight and stirring escapes told by old people whose eyes light up as they recall incidents of the past which had been handed down from generation to generation.

One incident concerned George Miller, who used to be quite a well-known character in Christchurch, and who once lived in the old Priory gatehouse and in the Mill on Christchurch Quay.

He was returning through the fir wood from Boscombe Chine, where he had been helping to unload a cargo of brandy. With a black mask over his face and carrying two kegs on his chest and two on his back, he was labouring home when he came to close quarters with two gobloos. George, a man of over six feet, threw off his assailants — and his kegs — then in a fierce struggle brought both officers down. He bound them hand and foot, re-shouldered his kegs, and went home to bed. The gobloos were found next morning.

When the brandy had been landed and carried to the customers it still had to be coloured and made ready for sale, and one old lady of Christchurch described how this was done,

> "When I was a girl," she said, "Father would go out after dark in his great pea jacket with a dark lantern strapped in his belt, and then in the early morning I would hear them come in with the kegs.
>
> "There was a great stone in the middle of our kitchen, and underneath it a great hole full of water, into which the kegs were sunk, and when we had an opportunity, we got them out and watered the brandy down, putting in burnt sugar to give it a dark colour. We always had to light a bonfire and burn old boots in front of the house to make a smell, and so disguise

the smell of the brandy, which was so strong you could smell it all down the street."

An old resident of Christchurch used to go round with a baker's cart, and he would carry a large basket containing bottles of brandy and Hollands covered with a loaf or two on the top.

Different names were used as passwords to describe the goods to the customers. For instance, when he went to a dairy at Iford he had to enquire if they wanted any milk. If the reply was in the affirmative he would ask,

"Do you want it from the white cow or the brown?"

At another place it was,

"Will you have the White Ensign or the Union Jack?" — the white ensign being 'Hollands'; for other customers the passwords were 'Lobsters' or 'Crabs'.

One of the last smuggling runs to take place in Christchurch was in 1876 according to Mr. Russell Oakley who said,

> "So far as is known, the last tubs of brandy smuggled into Christchurch were brought by road from Lymington on Christmas Eve of that year. It was a small consignment divided amongst a few of the tradespeople, some of whom, alive today (c. 1942) have vivid recollections of the share out and its results.
>
> "The late Mr. Tom Clark, who took part in the share-out, always declared that he could not remember any Christmas when Christmas Carols were so fervently sung by adults at Purewell Cross!"

The Black House, Mudeford

9

Keystone under the Hearth

"AH", said an old fisherman of about eighty years as he smacked his lips and then roared with laughter at the thought of the Preventer being outwitted — "nothing tastes half as good as that stuff did!"

The Preventer or Preventive Officer was always busy trying to catch the smugglers who used the routes from Barton Cliffs, Highcliffe or Mudeford which led inland to Picket Post, Burley, and into the New Forest.

John King of Burley was a man who remembered smuggling days. He was "a big man like a gnarled oak, hard as iron" and he had many times taken "a couple of Forest ponies with sacks on their backs and had gone down to the sea". He said that the smugglers' route was "across Cranes Moor, up the 'Smugglers' Path', through Vereley and Ridley, up to Smugglers' Road there, and on to Fritham".

It would seem that John King, even as an old man, was still active "with the Gentlemen", and he would bring kegs of brandy all the way from Barton Cliffs to a hiding place cleverly concealed "under the hearth".

The smugglers would say,

> "Keystone under the hearth," and
> "Keystone under the horse's belly."

This meant that the contraband was hidden either under flag stones by the fire or under the floor or stones where the horses were stabled.

Another story tells of a quantity of contraband which was brought from Highcliffe past a certain Sally Cox's cottage to Crow Hill. It is also probable that there was a smugglers' walk which led over Poor Man's Common to Picket Post, and it has been suggested that there is still a bricked up cellar somewhere beneath the bracken.

A difficult area of ground to cover when being pursued by the preventive men was the open heath land at Thorney Hill. During one hot chase the horses and a waggon load of goods were driven straight into the great barn at Chubb's or possibly Atkin's Farm at Burley.

The farmer there pretended that he had been bowled over by the waggon and that his leg was broken by the impact when the preventive men questioned him as to the whereabouts of the free traders, and he went on to tell them that if they rode hard they would perhaps catch up with the free traders further on in the village of Burley.

Cargoes landed at Lymington, Milford and Milton were often taken up the Boldre River to the New Forest and Becton and Chewton bunnies, which were convenient for the free traders from what was Slop Pond, now Highcliffe, and nearby to use.

Naish Farm, built on the cliffs at Milton, and commanding views of the Isle of Wight, Christchurch Bay and the distant

Purbeck Hills, was in an excellent position for smugglers to survey the coast and make sure all was clear for a landing.

The farm,[†] a very old building, is mentioned in the Christchurch Cartulary. The so-called Manor of Naish (Ashe) and South Chewton once belonged to the Christchurch Priory. As early as 1596 it is recorded that "Richard Wigmore of Naish Farm and South Chewton paid rent of £13 16s. 0d.".

There is a tunnel leading to Chewton Glen from the outbuildings of the farm, but it is difficult to say whether it was used for the farm effluent or for the smugglers alone as an escape route to the glen.

No doubt many a cargo was hidden at the farm before being taken up Chewton Glen and away to the New Forest.

About the middle of the eighteenth century the ancient Manor House at Becton was burnt down. It has been suggested that this was due to a spark falling on to a keg of spirits which had been broached.

In a cottage at Milton lived Mr. Bursey,[*] one of the Christchurch Customs Officers. These officers were dubbed 'shingle-pickers' by the local people. There were many pitched battles between the army and the preventive men, and the free traders at Milton Green and in the surrounding district.

Mr. A. T. Lloyd, a local historian, writing in the Ashleon Magazine, quotes the following from the Hampshire Chronicle, which was founded in the 1770's:—

> 'A most shocking murder was committed on Thursday night of the 24 ult. (Aug., 1780) at Milton. A gang of smugglers went to the house of Mr. John Bussey (*probably Bursey*), officer of the Customs, and calling him up, beat him in a most inhuman manner, particularly on the head, so that 7 pieces were taken from his skull the next morning. His wife, looking out of the window and crying "Murder," one of the villians

† Not necessarily the same farm building as that standing today

* Mr. Bursey actually lived at Chewton, not Milton. He was brutally attacked by a gang of smugglers in 1780

fired a blunderbuss at her and swore if she did not go in they would come and murder her and her children.'

The New Milton Parish Records show that in June 1825 Dr. Quartley of Christchurch presented a bill for 'extracting a ball from Jas. Read,' and for examining his dead body three days later. Francis Fooks, an E. Lulworth youth, is mentioned in the burial records for Oct. 21, 1832 with a marginal note by the clergyman saying "shot in a smuggling transaction."

A story from the family of Mr. Kellaway, who died at Milton in 1934, tells of a Barton woman who had warned the preventive men of an expected landing of brandy. She was afterwards found to have been asphyxiated whilst she slept. It seems that her windows, doors and chimney had been sealed with blankets. Certainly a grim story from the smuggling past!

Mr. A. Cole, in "Recollections of Milford" (Vol. 2 No. 5) says that he remembered his grandfather, who was born in 1797, pointing out a spot in a lane leading from Ashley to Barton Common where he saw two dragoons, who were chasing some smugglers, floundering in the mire. The smugglers escaped. Another time, he saw the Riding Officer's horse tied to a post on Milford Cliff, near where the Victoria Hotel used to stand. While the Officer was standing some distance away, a smuggler crept up and cut the saddle girths, thus preventing him from giving chase.

According to the local people, "Paddy's Gap" was used by the free traders for landing contraband. This may well have been true, for this lonely and beautiful part of the coast between Barton and Milford would have been ideal for the smugglers.

10

In the New Forest

SMUGGLERS used to meet at the *Queen's Head,* a seventeenth century inn at Burley. Recently a hidden cellar was discovered underneath the Stable Bar at the inn. Old coins, bottles and pistols found there suggest that it was used as a secret hiding place when the free traders were hard pressed by the excisemen. An old yew tree in Pound Lane, Burley, was known as the 'Dockyard', and here the ponies were left whilst the contraband was being delivered or hidden away.

In the *Queen's Head* the smugglers would make their plans for handling cargoes expected at Chewton Bunny, a miniature gorge where a stream runs down from the Forest to the sea at Highcliffe.

This was a most convenient landing place for goods destined for Burley, Ringwood, Fordingbridge and Salisbury. The contraband was brought up in waggons and on horseback along the track from the head of the Bunny over Chewton Common to the *Cat and Fiddle Inn* at Hinton, where the men would unload some of their tubs.

According to legend the *Cat and Fiddle,* one of the oldest roadside inns in the county, was, years before the smugglers frequented it, the last place of call for the pilgrims and wayfarers on the west boundary of the New Forest. According to the book "Annals of Ytene" by D. M. Northcroft, it is possible that a building on the present site was used by the Saxons as a hostelry and the name may have been a rough translation of "Catherine la Fidele," wife of Peter the Great. Mr. A. T. Lloyd says that it has certainly been known as the "Cat and Fiddle" since 1754. There was an astonishing amount of traffic in illicit goods over this route during the heyday of smuggling. In one period of three months the customs of smuggling. In one period of three months the customs officers at Christchurch received from the Award Court of Southampton rewards totalling £238 for goods confiscated at Burley and Hinton.

In 1803, Riding Officer Abraham Pike wrote in his journal:

"I surveyed the coast to Bourn, and, being informed by Mr. Newman that he had seized a waggon and about 70 casks of spirits in a common near Shirley (*north of Hinton*), and that he was afterwards attacked by several persons unknown (*by whom*) the waggons and goods were rescued, and that he had made a private mark on the waggon and could swear to it, I set out with my Riding Officers and a party of the Royal Horse Artillery in pursuit of it to Shirley, Sanford, Kingston Haven. Searched several suspected places. No success."

Later, however, this zealous officer recovered the goods and identified the waggon by the mark, and the smugglers were brought to justice.

Transportation or hanging were the severest penalties for this offence, and they generally preferred the latter.

By the roadside at Mark Way near Wilverley Post, surrounded by a protective fence, stands on the lonely heath the insignificant remains of what was once a great tree known as the Naked Man. From its stout boughs many malefactors, highwaymen as well as smugglers, paid the penalty of their wrongdoings at the end of the hangman's rope, so it is said, although it is not known to be a legal hanging tree.

Smuggling was an activity usually carried on by the men, whilst their womenfolk were content to stay at home and welcome any contraband that came their way to help to keep down the housekeeping bills. There were, however, some women who delighted in actually taking part in the excitement and profit of the illicit trade.

One of these was Lovey Warne, a high spirited girl who, with her brothers Peter and John, occupied a cottage by the smugglers' path at Knave's Ash, between Crow and Burley.

This enterprising young woman and her brothers successfully eluded the excise men, for they knew every inn and hiding place in the area. Lovey took her part in the actual smuggling, and under the very noses of the customs officers many a length of silk or lace was pertly carried off wrapped round her shapely body beneath her clothes.

Her chief task, however, was to warn the free-traders during the day time of the presence of the Riding Officers. Dressed in a cloak of the brightest scarlet, she would stand, whenever danger threatened, at the top of Vereley Hill, close to Picket Post. From this point of vantage she was clearly visible to the smugglers at almost every approach to Burley.

By night, the signal was the responsibility of Murphy and Charles Bromfield, who would hang a warning lantern at the top of the tallest oak tree close to their cottage on Vereley Hill.

Lovey joined in many of her brothers' smuggling escapades, and it has been said that on these occasions she would "tuckup her skirts and ride astride with two flagons of spirits slung across her pony".

In spite, or perhaps because, of this careless abandon to the spirit of the occasion in her youth, she maintained her health and strength to help the smugglers right into old age, and her name is remembered to this day in the New Forest.

The Cat and Fiddle Inn, Hinton

11

Buckler's Hard

THE yachtsman, sailing from Lepe up the winding tidal waters of the Beaulieu River past St. Catherine's Creek, Gin's Bank, and along Fiddler's Reach to Buckler's Hard, may not realise that he is taking the same course used by the smugglers over two hundred years ago.

The Free Traders rowed with muffled oars on the night tide, and unshipped their contraband on the solitary shores of a grass-fringed backwater. Then, their task over, they went their quiet ways to Buckler's Hard to divide their payment among themselves over a mug of ale or brandy at the smugglers' den, little knowing that this would be a meeting place of a very different kind — namely a chapel — in the twentieth century.

At Buckler's Hard, between 1745 and 1822, no less than fifty-six warships, as well as a number of merchant ships, were built. Here, in 1781, Henry Adams constructed Nelson's famous flagship the *Agamemnon,* of 64 guns. It was whilst Nelson was commanding this ship that he lost the sight of his right eye during an engagement on Corsica. Later, under another captain, the vessel took part in the glorious Battle of Trafalgar.

A gay, roistering crowd celebrated the launching of any vessel at this yard, and hundreds of people with their waggons and horses came from miles around to cheer the ship as she slipped down to the waters of the river.

Fine French brandy, smuggled in the false bottoms of the carts, flowed freely among the labourers and shipbuilders on these festive occasions.

Buckler's Hard is preserved for us today amid the green grass and tall trees of the English countryside, where the forest ponies ramble and graze freely over a single broad street, bordered by two rows of orderly red brick cottages, leading to the quay and the pleasant waters of the Beaulieu River.

To H. V. Morton it appeared,

> "A ghostly place! When the last slipway cracks and falls into the water, I would like to think that some old native will see, faint as if spun in mist on Beaulieu River, a gallant ship, her sails glimmering, her colours shot to shreds, come creeping home to Buckler's Hard to fade like a night fog into the English grass which gave her birth."

12

Tom Johnstone

1772 - 1839

AS a young Hampshire fisher-lad of a mere nine years, Tom Johnstone must have found life a splendid game, and his playgrounds were probably the lonely salt marshes of Lymington, with their channels leading to the curling surf of the sea.

He enjoyed a carefree life and was unworried by the taxes, wars and poor living which plagued his elders. He lived with his widowed mother and grew up helping his fisherman uncle, Georgie Hammond. He mended nets, scraped and cleaned his uncle's small boat and went out fishing with him.

Although it was hard for a fisherman to make a living, there were times when food was plentiful at home. When the smugglers landed their contraband, then money, drink and food were freely bestowed on their families.

Tom, hidden in the shadows, watched these landings at Shore Head, south of Lymington and Pennington. He had followed the free-traders and had seen them take their ponies and carts to Pennington Marsh Gate. There they waited to receive the load of brandy which the rest of the men, wearing mud-pattens, dragged over the mud flats in flat-bottomed boats, to the firm land.

There were times when Tom saw the Preventive Officers closing on the smugglers. He ran to warn the men that the 'searchers' were nearby. The smugglers hurriedly trod the kegs into the soft mud and escaped.

When all was well and the landing went smoothly, Tom followed the waggons and pack-horses over the rough cart tracks which led to the old 'Marl' pit at Bowers Copse where many a hundred tubs were hidden and well camouflaged with brush wood.

Tom knew all about the press gangs, too. No young man was safe when they were about. These hated tyrants lurked in the shadows and crept up behind a man, seized him, and took him away to serve in one of His Majesty's ships with no chance to say farewell to his family.

Because Tom had spent the years since the age of nine in the fishing and smuggling trade, he knew the South Coast well, and particularly the Hampshire shores. Before he was twenty-one his reputation as a Channel Pilot was widespread.

Being a young man of enterprise and spirit, and desirous of helping his country to fight the French, he joined a British Privateer, *The Three Friends* from Gosport. This ship was captured by the enemy and he was imprisoned in a filthy dungeon in France.

By agreeing to take a secret package from his captors to a French spy in Southampton, he obtained his release from prison, and sailed in a smuggling lugger to England. During this voyage the ship was boarded by men of the British cruiser *Defiance*, and they searched it for contraband.

By a clever scheme, Tom managed to pass the secret package to the midshipman in command of the boarding party. The package was delivered to Captain Nicholas Mowbray, R.N. The contents of the package proved to be most valuable to His Majesty's Government. Unfortunately, during this episode Tom was injured in the right arm. The lugger was allowed to sail on its way to England.

Once on shore, Johnstone found himself in another dilemma. He was caught by a Pressing Officer from whose clutches he escaped after a fierce fight, and thus became a deserter from the Royal Navy.

Tom went into hiding in Sussex where he organised a highly successful band of 'gentlemen' and made a considerable profit from smuggling. During these exploits, and just when he was considering moving on to fresh and less dangerous grounds in Kent, he met Sir Robert Goodhurst of Goodhurst Grange, Sussex.

Sir Robert Goodhurst persuaded Tom to smuggle to France some 'V.I.P. cargo', namely a certain General Barrère who was then a prisoner of war in this country.

General Barrère, an expert in Mediteranean strategy, had agreed to act in France as an agent for the British.

Under the guise of a 'Big Run', and at great personal risk, Johnstone carried out the task assigned to him. When he returned after this achievement his luck ran out and he was captured by a zealous Riding Officer at Winchelsea after landing a tremendous load of contraband.

Tom was unable to disclose his secret activities and he was thrown into the New Gaol in London.

In 1798 he escaped from prison, undoubtedly aided by the advice of his defence counsel, Serjeant Simon Colepeper, who was sent to him possibly by someone with influence in the government. Mr. Colepeper suggested that he could not do better than bribe his warders and thus escape. This Tom accomplished.

Once free again Johnstone then served his country by offering himself as a Pilot to the British forces which were to be sent to Holland. His offer was accepted by the British Government. Sir Ralph Abercromby, who was in command of these forces, was so pleased with the efficient way in which Tom had carried out his duties that he was fully pardoned for his past mis-deeds.

During his visit to Holland he met Colonel Cornelius Ten Brink and his wife Frederika at Nordwinkel Farm about five miles to the south east of Helder. Frederika fell in love with the dashing 'Captain' Thomas Johnstone. Incidentally, the title 'Captain' was bestowed upon him by his friends. Tom never used the term with regard to himself.

Carried away by success and his infatuation with Frederika, he lived such a life of reckless extravagance that again he reverted to smuggling, always successfully evading the Revenue Officers. Unfortunately what the customs men couldn't do, his inability to pay his bills did do, and in 1802 he was captured and imprisoned in the debtors' Prison of the Fleet in London.

Once more Serjeant Colepeper advised Tom to escape from prison. Not only were the charges against him of smuggling and debt so great, but also the Marquess of Townwood, a rival for the love of Frederika and a highly influential person, wanted him out of the way. Transportation seemed inevitable for Tom if he stayed in prison to face his trial. Serjeant Colepeper promised to help by getting a message to Tom's friend Arthur Hudson, begging him to have transport ready day and night for him near the prison, at the end of Farringdon Street, should his escape prove successful.

It was wretched, windy and raining miserably when Tom made his escape. About twenty four hours after Mr. Colepeper had left, Tom loosened the bolts of the prison doors and crept from his cell to scale the twenty foot prison wall. It was protected at the top with iron spikes and broken glass, and all this separated him from the outside world.

Once at the top of the wall Tom, completely exhausted and bruised by his efforts, rested in some great degree of discomfort, and tried to regain his strength. As he did so he looked downwards on the wet cobbles of the street beneath him. He spotted an iron projection about half way down the wall. This was a stout iron bracket holding a lantern which shone with a pale glimmering light in the pouring rain.

Johnstone considered the ironwork strong enough to hold him and he calculated that it would help his drop from the wall if he could first land on that bracket.

Johnstone, chilled to the bone and thoroughly wet, decided to take a chance. He dropped from the wall and fell on to the bracket. As he landed he tore his thigh from hip to knee on a jagged piece of the iron structure. He fought in terrible agony to keep his balance on the bracket, for just at that moment he heard the night watchman approach. Blood from his wound mingled with raindrops and spattered on the cobbles. The night watchman stopped, peered into the night and passed on his way.

Tom slipped off the bracket to the ground. In terrible pain and nauseating agony he crawled along the pavement to the sanctuary of Arthur Hudson's hackney coach at the corner of the street. Tom was tended by his friends as they rode in the coach. When they reached Wandsworth he was transferred to a post-chaise which took him to Brighton in the company of a surgeon who was, no doubt, repaid for his services with fine French brandy or tobacco.

A fast lugger took him to Calais where a French smuggler, grateful for past services, made Tom welcome and cared for him in his distress.

As he was convalescing a commandant of the French Army called to see him. Tom was reminded by the officer of the high reward waiting in England for anyone who found him. He also said that he could stay in France on condition that he would do something in return for that country.

Tom, ignorant of the task before him, agreed to discuss the matter in Paris with the Minister concerned with the project. Tom understood from his conversation in Paris that he would be carrying out some kind of smuggling in Holland and that he was to go to Flushing.

Johnstone asked for a few days' leave before embarking on this new venture. During that time he literally bumped into an American, Robert Fulton, a brilliant engineer who was studying the intricacies of the Marine Steam engine for the French Government.

The two men, in that short time, became close friends, and Tom spent much of his leave with Fulton in his drawing offices and visited the prototypes of the new ships powered by steam. Finally, Tom left for Flushing.

When he arrived there, he discovered that the special mission he had to carry out was to smuggle English gold from Southwold to Flushing, whence the gold would be transferred to Napoleon's empty coffers.

Johnstone carried out these gold runs during the latter part of the year 1802 and became very rich as a result of his activities. It was possible to carry out these operations successfully because of a lull in the fighting after the uneasy Peace of Amiens in March of that same year.

Unfortunately for Tom, in May 1803, England was suddenly at war with France again, and the gold runs were ended by order of the French Government. Ironically enough it is possible that, by this time, Napoleon had enough English gold to finance further his war against Britain. Johnstone was now in great difficulty. Unemployed in a hostile country and unwelcome in England, he found himself at the mercy of his enemies.

Bonaparte, knowing Tom's capabilities, offered him the chance of freedom and a sizeable reward if he would pilot a French invasion Fleet to the English coast. Tom was certainly not willing to do this for 'Old Boney' and to the offer he replied,

"I am a smuggler, but a true lover of my country and no traitor".

Napoleon immediately imprisoned him at Flushing. For the third time, and again he was lucky, Tom broke away from his guards at an opportune moment, jumped into the sea and swam to a ship which by chance was American, the *Lafayette* out of New Orleans. He was taken on board. Again he was in a difficult position, for America was hostile to Britain. However, he managed to talk his way into staying in the ship as they were shorthanded, so he escaped to America.

At New Orleans he introduced himself as a British Channel Pilot and served as a clerk to the British Consul there. During his short stay in America a pardon was granted to him for the second time, provided he returned to England in the *Roebuck* frigate. This he did.

Once in England he joined Robert Fulton. Together they carried out experiments at Dover Castle which involved testing explosives which were fixed to catamarans. These were to be used to blow up a ship from under the water. During the Walcheren Expedition, Tom took one of these "new fangled machines" to Calais Harbour, and though it exploded and caused confusion and damage amongst the anchored ships, it was regarded as suspect by the Royal Navy.

In the same Expedition in 1809 Tom carried out a brilliant and dangerous operation by swimming to the Flushing ramparts with an explosive big enough to destroy the enemy's powder magazine.

For his brave services Johnstone was granted an annual

pension of £100. Later he was given the command of H.M.S. *Fox*, a new revenue cruiser based at Plymouth.

Tom was a successful Captain, for, as an old smuggler, he was wise to the ways of the free traders. Because of this he was disliked by the smugglers, who called him a scurvy rat, and vowed to murder him at the first opportunity.

Recovering from a particularly vicious attack on his life one night in Plymouth, Tom reflected that he could see the points of view of both the Government and the Smugglers in the contraband cause. Nevertheless, he decided, he had always defied Governments and really felt that he would not make a perfect Government Officer. He therefore withdrew from the command of H.M.S. *Fox*.

After Tom's last successful sea fight with the moonshiners, during which he was badly slashed near the eyes, he was discharged honourably from the Navy. Thus, at the age of 44, he retired to a house in Vauxhall Bridge Road, London. He married Miss Constance Stonebridge, a Squire's daughter from Somerset, who bore him three children.

About five years after his marriage, Tom was visited by some of Bonaparte's close friends. They asked him to take their ex-Emperor from St. Helena to the United States. This he agreed to attempt, unperturbed by the obvious difficulties. He intended to carry out the rescue by using one of his inventions — a sub-marine vessel.

Plans were prepared, and this vessel, a boat of 100 ft. long, had masts and sails which could be lowered and stowed away. The idea was that, when danger loomed on the horizon, the boat would submerge and continue its journey under water.

Johnstone was offered a reward of £40,000 to be presented to him on the day that the boat set sail.

Napoleon put an end to this somewhat precarious projected journey, and to Johnstone's reward, because he died before the boat was finished. With customary aplomb Tom returned to his half-built boat and tried to sell it, but there were no buyers.

A year later the Spanish Government sent representatives to see the completed 'diving boat' in action. 'Captain' Johnstone with the Spaniards aboard, demonstrated his model in the Thames. Going from London Bridge to Blackwall he had some perilous moments, when, on submerging, the boat tangled with the cables of another vessel. Looking towards his Spanish companions, he observed unhurriedly that they had but two and a half minutes to live, unless they cleared the cables. By good fortune the vessel did, somewhat unceremoniously, right itself and appear on the surface of the water. In doing so, however, the observation port gave way and the interior filled with swirling mass of dirty water, muddy weed and other litter from the river.

The Spaniards did not buy the vessel.

During the latter part of his life Tom Johnstone lived quietly through changes from sail to steamship, and young Queen Victoria came to the throne.

His favourite pastime was, no doubt, to watch the shipping on the Thames and dream of days gone by.

In March, 1839, 'Captain' Thomas Johnstone died as he slept. A quiet ending to his sixty-nine years of turbulent and adventurous life.

* * * *

Mention has already been made of Mr. Cole (p.64). His grandfather saw a Press Gang chasing a man down the High St., Lymington. The Press Gang Headquarters are said to have been situated on the Quay in what is now known as "Pressgang Cottage". A plaque in front of the house states,

"The Old Harlequin Inn
Headquarters of the Press Gang circa 1800"

There is at the Town Hall, Lymington, a Press Gang Warrant of 11th March 1803 which was made out to "James Girrard Constable of the Borough of Lymington" and signed by the Mayor of Lymington, Rob: Allen. Part of it states:

" . . . We do hereby empower and direct you to impress as many Seamen, and Seafaring Men, of strong bodies and good health, as you possibly can procure, giving to each Man so Impressed One Shilling for Money . ."

Some interesting entries in Lymington Burial Registers include:

1781, Hugh Baggs, a sailor belonging to the Press Gang, from H.M. Storeship 'The Robinson', commanded by Lieut. Nath. Phillips.

Thomas Hanson, who died of his wounds received on board a smuggling lugger, in an engagement with the Rose Cutter. 1799 Charles Colborne, shot in the custom house boat, by smugglers.

13

Hookey's Hole

SOME may doubt whether Sam Hookey ever really existed, but certainly there were Hookeys in the Christchurch area, for in the Salisbury Journal of February 26th, 1759, it is reported that:

> "On Friday the 16th inst., about 12 o'clock at night, Messrs. Buffey, Hookey and Stokes, Riding Officers at Christchurch, after a desperate Engagement with the Smugglers, made a seizure of a Tun Weight of Green and Bohea Tea, which they secured and sent in the Yacht to the Custom House at Southampton."

It is not inconceivable that Sam was of the same family as the Riding Officer, but on the other side!

In a fanciful story by Mr. Ede England,† Sam Hookey's mother was a lovely Spanish girl who was kidnapped from Guernsey by a daring fisherman-smuggler on one of his ventures. Sam was the eldest of eleven children, and the family lived in a rough dwelling on the banks of the Stour at what is now the village of Wick, Bournemouth, in the early part of the eighteenth century.

From his earliest days, he displayed courage and daring

† It has come to light that the late Mr. Ede England, in a letter written in 1962, stated that he had written a story about Sam Hookey, to promote a local holiday camp, "which was based on no facts whatever".

beyond his fellows. He always had the bright ideas, and he always took the greatest risks.

One of his adventures nearly cut short his young life when he and his companions burrowed into one of the prehistoric burial mounds on Hengistbury Head, places which were looked on at that time with superstitious dread. Sam alone tunnelled to the heart of the mound, and as he scrambled back he was trapped by a great stone.

His terrified gang left him, and several hours elapsed before a casual passer-by happened to hear his cries and rescued him.

He learned the craft of the blacksmith, and is reputed to have had a smithy in Pound Lane, Christchurch. Throughout his career he was also a very successful smuggler, and no doubt his skill as a smith enable him to manufacture many tools of the smuggling trade, such as grappling hooks.

He spent his money freely and enjoyed life to the full, and, although he was called "The Wicked Man of Wick", he does not appear to have been either cruel or evil. He had a flair for leadership, and he was a good organiser.

One of his most successful ventures was carried out in Christchurch Harbour on a Whitsuntide night in 1764.

He divided his gang into two sections, one of which acted as a decoy party, landing brandy tubs on the shore by the Bourne River. This cargo was seized by the Riding Officer and his men after a very convincing show of force by the smugglers.

Only later did the excise men discover that the tubs were filled with sea water.

Meanwhile Sam, with three luggers in full sail, boldly entered Christchurch Harbour, sailed up to the marshy ground where Pontin's Holiday Camp now stands, and landed, it is said, no less than 12,033 tubs of spirits, two tons of tea, and five bales of silk — and not a shot was fired!

This venture has gone down into history as the largest single run on any coast in England.

Throughout his life, Hookey threw himself wholeheartedly into smuggling of all kinds, but on the night of the 29th of August, 1796, he ventured for the last time.

He was seventy-one years old, and still full of enterprise and daring, though his strength and judgement were failing, when he ran his last load. The contraband lace, tea and gold, was landed at Wick Ferry, close by the humble shack where he was born.

The smugglers were intercepted by the preventive men as they were fording the Stour, and during the confused fighting, Sam Hookey, heavily weighed down by the gold in the money belt wrapped round his body, slipped into a hole deep in the river bed and drowned. Neither his body nor the gold was ever recovered.

"There's treasure in Hookey's Hole for those who can find it — aye, gold, real gold". So said the old people of Wick, but when a team tried to find the gold in 1954, "nary a piece was found".

* * * *

There is evidence that a Christchurch gang of smugglers existed. William Arnold, Collector of Customs in the Isle of Wight always tried to keep a close watch on the activities of the most daring smugglers and many gangs were broken up. Arnold-Forster writes that:

> 'Of the Christchurch gang, George Hewson had been lodged in the Poole gaol, and Richard Coombes, Streeter and White at Winchester. In 1787, Arnold, in reporting the escape of the two latter, remarks that both were men of property.
>
> They are supposed to be now in the Island of Guernsey or Alderney, but occasionally return to the neighbourhood of Christchurch, where Streeter narrowly escaped from being taken by disguising himself in woman's clothes. He has a house near Christchurch where his wife still resides, and where he carries on a considerable tobacco manufactory. White rents and works a small farm there, more on pretence for keeping horses and wagons to assist in smuggling than for any real purpose of husbandry.'

Brandy tubs with stone sinkers

14

Bournemouth

TRAVELLING along the roads today, through the built-up areas which link Christchurch with Bournemouth and Poole, it seems almost incredible that only just over 100 years ago it was possible to walk from Poole to Christchurch without meeting a single soul.

"Oh, Bournemouth hasn't any history", has often been said. Well, perhaps it has not been established as long as the ancient boroughs of Christchurch and Poole, but, geographically speaking it is part of the same coast-line and the mouth of the Bourne has been noted in the Christchurch Cartulary of 1372 as "La Bournemowthe" (1407 Vol. II Folio 134), and on the first 1-inch ordnance map of 1811 it was known as Bourne Mouth.

Who knows what history lies silent under these shores? The footprints of the Iron Age Men who inhabited Hengistbury Head were once deep in the sands, and many a pretty maiden may have searched in vain amongst the pebbles for a lost brooch or ring. Where were the wattled huts of the Saxons or the rude homes of the Anglo-Norman fishermen built? For hundreds of years only the splashing oar of a solitary fisherman at sea and the cry of the heron in heavy flight broke the silence of the heathland.

In 1567, James, the sixth Baron Mountjoy, discovered mineral deposits buried under the turf and waste land. He established a copperas and alum works at Parkstone in Dorset. This was subsequently allowed to decay, and he died, a ruined man, in 1581. Alum Chine is a reminder of his unsuccessful venture.

Late in the 18th century Alum Chine was used as a convenient landing and hiding place for the illegal goods brought in from France by the free traders.

The heathland, now, of course, developed by the citizens of Bournemouth, was once ranged over by the smugglers stealthily bringing in their contraband brandy, tobacco, silks and laces. Adventure, fighting and intrigue once cloaked the whole area in mystery.

The present roads, now busy with traffic, were built over the old smugglers' tracks leading from the shores to the heath. So convenient were they, that on survey, no better routes could be found, and the modern roads follow them.

The land West of Christchurch extending to Poole, and the hinterland stretching for about six miles inland from the seashore at Bourn was generally called Bourn Heath. Mr. J. J. Nightingale of Seaborne Road, Pokesdown, who died in 1963 at the age of 86, was a member of an old established family of horse breeders and always referred to this area as Bourn Heath, as did his father before him.

The deceptively quiet coastline or heathland was likely to erupt into activity when an affray between the free traders, Excisemen and soldiers disturbed the chines and sandy paths with their pistol shots and their cries of pain, anger or derision.

The heathland had many secret hiding places for tubs amongst the furze, or for silks, laces and tea in special holes lined with wood or brick and disguised with grass or heather. Usually only those who knew the secrets of the heath could discover the forbidden contraband.

These hiding places were certainly well kept from the continually searching eyes of the Riding Officer and his men. The area of heathland was so great that the officers were just not able to comb it thoroughly, but even so, they did uncover considerable hoards of contraband.

Mr. Abraham Pike, Riding Officer of Excise for Christchurch, whose district was from Hurst Castle to Poole, reported one particular day in his journal for 1803-1804. He said:

> "Oct 13 1803 At my Residence Corresponded with Mr Wise Called on By Msfs Preston Jones & Wise informing us the smugglers was working at Bourn Set out with my Officers Mr Wise and a Party of the 20 Regt of Light Dragoons to Bourn at Bourn and in the Heath found and seized 63 Casks of Foreign Spirits and one cask of Tobacco in Company with the above officer and Party at Bourn met Mr Buck Landwaiter and his Boats Crew and corresponded from thence with Mr Wise Bacon & Newman to Poole with the seizure secured it in his Majesty's Warehouse Corresponded with the Comptroller on our return called and examined work (?) Book Surveyed the Coast home with Mr Bacon and Newman in the Heath near Kingston found and seized 2 Cases of Cordials 1 Cask of spirits and a small parcel of Tobaccos in Company with Mr Bacon and Newman Secured it at my Residence." (Christchurch).

This heathland, so near to Poole and Christchurch, yet so remote and wild, was an ideal landing place not only for contraband, but also for the soldiers of an invading enemy to land, and during the wars with the French, Napoleon could have thought that this would be the place for an invasion.

The Government recognised this threat and by all possible means prepared to meet any aggressor by building Martello Towers along the South Coast, and some kind of fort was built off the shores of Bournemouth. Roads bearing the name 'Martello' can be seen at Canford today.

The barracks at Christchurch, built on the orders of Gen. Sir Oliver de Lancey in 1795, housed Dragoons who, with their Artillery, could be despatched to the defence of Christchurch Bay, or to assist the Riding Officer of Customs and Excise.

The area was defended under the command of Captain Lewis D. G. Tregonwell of the Dorset Yeomanry throughout the years 1796 to 1802.

This man, whose portrait now hangs in the Council Chamber of the Town Hall, Bournemouth, was known as the 'Founder of Bournemouth'. He became thoroughly familiar with all parts of the Heathland, for, not only was he on the lookout for Frenchmen, but also for the smugglers who frequented the chines and inland hiding places.

It is generally understood that he so loved this area at the mouth of the Bourne that, after his second marriage to Henrietta Portman, of Bryanston in 1800, he decided to buy 8½ acres of this wild land. The cost then was £179.11.0 for this amount of land! In 1810 he then built thereon a mansion which was later known as Exeter House. Today it stands with the rest of the buildings known as the Exeter Hotel.

A plaque acknowledging the founder is on a wall at the hotel entrance:

"To the memory of
LEWIS D. G. TREGONWELL
who erected the first house in Bournemouth
on this site in 1810.
He died on January 18th 1832 aged 73 and was buried
in St. Peter's Churchyard, Bournemouth.
He was descended from Sir John Tregonwell
A member of an ancient Cornish family."

It is strange to think that this now prosperous and orderly seaside town, with its Churches, flats, houses and shops, stands where many men shepherded kegs of brandy to hiding places across the Heath and took them on their way to such market towns as Ringwood, Wimborne and Salisbury. I wonder how much the town owes to these 'departed spirits'.

* * * *

In about 1923, Mr. H. E. Lavender of The Mount, Moorlands Road, West Moors, was mending a chicken house at the end of the garden, which had been reclaimed from heathland. His foot broke through into a small cavity about 18" deep and rather less across. It was neatly lined with upright wooden planks. There was, alas, no brandy in it!

15

Isaac Gulliver

ONE of the most colourful and likeable smugglers was Isaac Gulliver, who was born at Thorney Down, near Chettle in 1745. He lived for many years in Howe Lodge, West Howe, Kinson near Bournemouth. This was a many-roomed gabled house which boasted secret chambers and possibly a tunnel leading to the coast at Poole. The house was demolished a year or two ago to make room for new road developments over the land where, from dark beaches, Isaac Gulliver's men led their pack horses laden with wines and spirits.

Mr. William Veal, a timber merchant, who was the last inhabitant of the house, said that to demolish the house had been a tragedy, for it meant that a piece of living history had gone. He said that it was a strange house and reputed to have been haunted by 'Old Gulliver's Ghost', but he had never seen or heard it.

Isaac Gulliver was a smuggler chief of medium stature, and fine build. His eyes were blue and he had clear-cut features. In the museum at Wimborne, Dorset, he is pictured wearing a powdered wig, yellow neckerchief, blue coat with brass or gold buttons and dark blue breeches.

Gulliver employed some sixty or so men, and he made sure that they were cared for and well treated. They were extremely loyal to their chief. He saw that they were well dressed and he provided them with a livery — which was not a uniform — to wear instead of their own poor clothing, and this was worn by his seamen smugglers as well as his land smugglers.

Men in his service had to grow their hair long and he provided them with hair powder, which was then a taxed commodity, so that they looked as though they were the retainers of a wealthy house. This custom led to his men being known as 'White Wigs'.

Gulliver's outstanding ability was to organise his men and resources to their very best advantage. So well did he control his affairs that in 1763, this capable young man evaded the Customs duties and brought contraband to the tune of £20,000 per year into the South Coast at such points as Lyme Regis, Weymouth, Poole and Canford as well as the Heath at Bourne.

He was a courageous, fearless and adventurous man, who was respected by all who had any contact with him. He was fair and just in his dealings, and although his clashes with Excise men were infrequent, he was proud of the fact that his employees had never mortally wounded an Officer in an affray, and he became known as 'The Gentle Smuggler'.

One of the highlights of his career was to lead the removal of thousands of pounds worth of merchandise from the beach at the mouth of the Bourne in a procession at least two miles long across the heathland to strong points at such inland towns as Dorchester, Wimborne, Fordingbridge, Ringwood or Salisbury, that at Wimborne being the *Kings Arms Hotel* at Eastbrook. He used to drop off his contraband at certain selected farms and the goods would be stored in secret cellars and vaults. He is thought to have owned or had access to farms dotted along these routes as far inland as Salisbury, where he could hide his goods and safely rest his pack horses by day.

In fact Isaac Gulliver owned a considerable amount of property. As well as Howe Lodge there was the High House at East End, Corfe Mullen — a tall narrow house built, so the story goes, so that Gulliver could see through the windows on either side and spot any approaching Excisemen in good time, so that he could escape to safety. He owned several properties in Wimborne, together with Longham Farm at Hampreston, Manor Farm at West Moors and Eggardon Farm or Eggardon Manor near Dorchester.

He bought Eggardon Farm in 1776 from William Chaffin of Chettle, and on some high land he grew a copse which was clearly visible from the sea. It has been reported that this was grown principally as a guide to his boats. The Excise authorities later ordered the trees to be cut down.

It is extraordinary that he should have escaped the authorities with such good effect, and so often — although to attack such a well armed convoy would have been a difficult matter for a Riding Officer unless he was well supported by the army, which was not much in evidence at the time.

On the other hand, it has been suggested that Gulliver

enjoyed a certain amount of freedom for his exploits because the Government were glad of his services to obtain information from France when normal communications were cut owing to the war. Indeed it has been inferred that he was able to warn the Government that George III's life was endangered by a French plot threatening to kill him.

Gulliver avoided being captured by the Excisemen many times, and the following example of his escapades has been recorded as being quite true.

The Preventive men were close on the heels of Gulliver when he managed, by the skin of his teeth, to get into his house. A week later the men returned with a warrant for his arrest. They knocked and demanded admittance to the house. They were answered by a woman with a mournful countenance. She told them that Gulliver had died only the day before and now he lay in his coffin. Doubting the woman's word, they demanded to be taken upstairs.

The Excisemen entered the bedroom, and to their dismay, for people in those days were terrified of being in the presence of the dead, there was Gulliver lying white and still in his coffin. Not only were they they shocked to see this, but their warrant was useless, for they could not arrest a dead man. They went away. The 'funeral' took place later, and the coffin, heavily weighted, was duly buried.

What about Gulliver's 'corpse'? It revived rapidly when the officers had gone and he washed the chalk from his hands and face then sat down to a hearty meal!

Gulliver became a wealthy man, for his exploits had served him well, and, in 1782 he received the King's Pardon and became a respectable citizen. One of his last ventures was into the wine and spirit business as a licensed trader, when no doubt he sold the goods from the vast stores which he had accumulated throughout his years of free-trading.

He sold his pack animals by auction, and they fetched high prices. The money that he had gained by his extraordinary capabilities was put out at interest, and, in fact, he became a money lender.

Further respectability came to Gulliver when his daughter Elizabeth was married to a certain Mr. William Fryer of Lytchett Minster and Wimborne, who was a banker. They lived in West Borough, Wimborne, in the house now used as offices by the Urban Council. Mr. Fryer established a Bank under the title of Fryer, Andrews, Woolfrey and Co. This was later known as the Wimborne Bank, then the Wimborne and Blandford Bank, and later still the Wimborne, Poole and Blandford Bank. Today it is a Branch of the National Provincial Bank.†

This family's name has been perpetuated by a monument in Kinson Churchyard, erected in 1915.

Gulliver's son Isaac died in 1798 at the age of 24. He was unmarried. Gulliver's grand-daughter, Ann Fryer, married Edward Castleman of Chettle. This couple lived at *Dormers* in East Borough, Wimborne.

Edward Castleman became a partner in a bank which opened on the premises, now occupied by a chemist, at the corner of Mill Lane, Wimborne, under the title of Dean, Castleman and Adams in 1820.

† The National Provincial Bank has since merged with the Westminster Bank.

Later this bank was bought by, or absorbed into, the Wilts & Dorset Bank in 1841. Other premises for this bank were built in the Square, and eventually it became a branch of Lloyds Bank.

Isaac Gulliver became a Churchwarden of Wimborne Minster, and, with a life of excitement and thrilling adventure behind him, died on the 13th September 1822, at No. 21 West Borough, Wimborne. His burial in Wimborne Minster gave the final mark of respectability to his boisterous life.

Hampshire, Wiltshire and Dorset all have possible links with Gulliver's past, for there are many cottages and farms which bear his name, and, on Parkstone Bay the very appellation, Lilliput, could very well set the seal to his connections with the area.

16

Kinson

SOME of the tracks from the shores of Bourne Chine led across the heathlands to the green fields and quiet winding lanes of Kingston, or Kinson as it is known today.

This lonely village with its little church tucked away behind the heath in what is now North Bournemouth, was ideally situated as a hide-out for the smugglers who were escaping from the Riding Officers and their men.

Kinson Church is spoken of widely nowadays as 'The Smugglers' Church'. It has a large tomb by the entrance porch and the marks on the tomb-stone are supposed to have been made by the free-traders when they hid their merchandise in the tomb.

The parapet on the Church Tower has grooves in the stone which resulted from the constant traffic of the ropes hauling the kegs of brandy, bales of tobacco or parcels of tea up to the safety of the tower. All this activity seems to have taken place as a matter of course and no one appears to have been captured here, so secret were the activities of these men. The average villagers in those days had a real fear of death and would not readily go near a churchyard at night. Of course there were many inhabitants who were on the side of the smugglers and they felt that an extra ration of tea or tobacco was ample reward for a little silence on their part.

It is quite possible that these free-traders were employed by Isaac Gulliver. One of the gang who used to hide contraband in the churchyard lies buried there. He was Robert Trotman. The inscription on his ivy-covered tombstone tells a sad story. Was he, for once, not guilty of smuggling when he was shot by an excise-man? Or do the words on his tombstone mean that the villagers quite openly regarded smuggling as a perfectly respectable way of life, and to be killed under such circumstances was to be murdered?

The words are:

> "To the memory of Robert Trotman, late of Roud (Rowde) in the county of Wilts, who was barbarously murdered on the shore near Poole, the 24th March 1765.
>
> "A little tea, one leaf I did not steal,
> For guiltless bloodshed I to God appeal;
> Put tea in one scale, human blood in t'other
> And think what 'tis to slay a harmless brother."

Robert Trotman came from Roud (Rowde) near Devizes in Wiltshire. He was believed to have been one of the 'Wiltshire Moonrakers'.

This name 'Moonrakers', was given to a group of smugglers who, one night when the moon was full, were raking up a number of kegs which had previously been hidden in the bed of a stream. While they were busy doing this, some men passed by and asked what they were doing at such an hour of the night. "Why", they said pointing to the reflection of the moon, "We be tryin' to get that there cheese out o' the water".

The men walked on, laughing at the simplicity of the local folks. It has been suggested that these passers-by were Excise-men. If so, who then, were the simpletons?

The army were also at a great disadvantage when chasing smugglers and Mr. Russell Oakley's story of Lord Shaftesbury and Mr. Hooper, the owner of Heron Court, illustrates this:

> 'The main road inland from Christchurch in those days was not what is known now as the Bournemouth Road. It left the town in a northerly direction and passed in front of Heron Court and then along a narrow lane coming out at Wimborne. In 1780 His Lordship, who was Chairman of the Customs and Excise, and Mr. Hooper were sitting down at dinner. Suddenly an immense clatter in front of the house disturbed the meal and it was ascertained that the noise was made by six or seven waggons, heavily loaded with kegs, (which) rushed past at a gallop. Lord Shaftesbury jumped up to look at the sight from the windows of the mansion, but the old squire sat quite still with his back to the window, and refused to turn round or look out. Soon afterwards a detachment of cavalry arrived with other horses, and the officer in charge dismounted and enquired at Heron Court which way the smugglers had gone. No one could tell them, and the squire politely said he had seen nothing'.

Smugglers' spout lantern

17

The Custom House of Poole

FROM the seventeenth to the nineteenth centuries Poole, together with Dartmouth and the Channel Islands was the Mother Port of the Newfoundland fishing fleet.

The Custom House at Poole was built about 1730 on a site closer to the quay than that occupied by the present day building. It was then owned by the principal port official, the Collector, who leased it to the Crown for periods of 21 years.

In his report to the Commissioners of Customs in London in 1773, the Collector said that its site was "certainly the most convenient place for one in this Port, being situated about the Centre of the Keys, and no vessel can come into the Harbour within Brownsea but the Surveyor can see her from his office".

The Custom House building usually contained a Long Room, so named by Christopher Wren in 1671, where the main public business was transacted, and was by tradition, on the first floor, as it is at Poole. The ground floor was used for the weighing business, the King's Warehouse and the Waterguard Service.

The Librarian of H.M. Customs and Excise at Poole gives a description from the Patent Rolls of Richard II, which,

> "might very well be the exact description of the Custom House in which Geoffrey Chaucer himself worked and speaks of a *domus pro tronagio,* a ground floor weigh-house, or floor for the weighing business and over that *a domus pro dicto computatorio,* or a first floor counting house plus (a Chaucerian touch, this) *quandam camerulam pro latrina dicto computatoris annexam,* or a certain little chamber adjoining the counting house for use as a latrine".

Poole Custom House was, and is now designed on similar lines. In the forecourt was a Medieval Beam used for weighing goods on which the King's Customs were to be charged. Poole alone of all this country's ports has the ancient King's Beam still standing on its ancient site, a reminder of Poole's former greatness as a port.

By 1797, however, a report to the Honourable Commissioners stated that the building was "so very old and in such a decayed state that the Long Room and Store Room over the same are supported by props".

Some improvements were made in 1803 and an adjacent private house was converted to office use. Outside there was considerable congestion whenever vessels were loading or discharging, for there was only room for one carriage to pass on the Quay, all of which made it difficult for goods to be weighed at the King's Scales and even to get into the Custom House.

Ten years afterwards, on the 22nd April, a report to the Board signed by David Lander, Collector, and Edward Allen, Comptroller, stated: "a most destructive fire broke out this morning near the Custom House . . ." This set light to the Custom House and several adjoining houses and stores. The public books were thrown out on to the quay in the "utmost confusion". The adjacent warehouse where the fire broke out contained "Naval Stores".

After complications with the Board and the Corporation of Poole, who had secured part of the land which included the site of the burnt Custom House, for a widening scheme, the new building was completed between 1813 and 1814 approximately on the same site as the earlier buildings.

The Customs were pleased with the buildings but the Collector was not happy about the "tenant's furniture and fittings". As time went on the refurnishing and refitting was completed — "even to the satisfaction of David Lander, the Collector", who remained the official in charge for over thirty years from his first appointment. He left the service in 1840.

The frontage of the Customs House is a replica of the town's older Guildhall, which is no longer used for Municipal affairs.

18

The Hawkhurst Gang

WHILST we tend to regard the smugglers of this period as romantic rascals who, whilst they undoubtedly broke the laws of the land, were not fundamentally vicious and evil, nevertheless, there were those who can only be described as villainous desperados, for whom smuggling was only a part of their general brutal lawlessness.

There can be little sympathy for such as these, who fully merited the utmost severity of punishment which the law imposed.

Such was the Hawkhurst Gang from Sussex, an exceptionally wicked band of smugglers under the leadership of Thomas Kingsmill.

These men terrorised the people of Kent and Sussex during the first half of the eighteenth century. So outrageous were their deeds that in 1747 the people banded together to protect themselves. The 'Goudhurst Band of Militia' was formed by the people of the village of that name under the leadership of Sturt, a man who had served in the army.

The group planned to thwart the gang and to bring them to justice. Unhappily, the Hawkhurst Gang attacked and seized one of the Militia and forced him to disclose the plan.

The smugglers then declared war on the people of Goudhurst, and threatened to murder them and burn down their village. Sturt at once mobilised his forces to meet the gang, who promptly opened fire on the villagers. A battle developed, and finally the Hawkhurst Gang retreated, pursued by the Militia.

The *Gentlemen's Magazine* of April 1747 reports:

> "Two smugglers, George Kinsman and Barnet Wollit, both outlaws, the first of which formerly killed a man on Hurst Green, were killed in a skirmish with the townsmen of Goudhurst in Kent, who found it necessary to arm against these desperadoes, who rob and plunder and live upon the spoil wherever they come."

The leader of the gang, Thomas Kingsmill, a native of Goudhurst, escaped, and eventually turned up again with his men in Poole, Dorset.

Thirty-seven hundredweight of tea, worth £500, and intended to be landed on the coast of Sussex, was in the vessel intercepted and captured by Captain William Johnson on its way from Guernsey.

Captain Johnson was cruising in the Poole Revenue Cutter when he sighted the smuggling cutter, *The Three Brothers*. For seven hours he chased her, and finally caused her to heave to after firing on her.

On board, the Captain found the tea in oilskin and canvas bags. There were also thirty-nine casks of brandy and rum, and a small bag of coffee. This contraband was impounded in Poole Custom House on Poole Quay.

The smugglers, furious at this interference in their plans, met in Charlton Forest, and, joined by Kingsmill and the Hawkhurst Gang, decided to remove the tea by force from the Custom House.

On the 6th October, 1747, at night, whilst thirty men, heavily armed with pistols, carbines and blunderbusses, guarded the roads leading to Poole, another thirty, also heavily armed, rode down a little back lane in Poole leading to the Custom House, dismounted, and proceeded to attack the building.

Using hatchets and iron bars, they forced open four doors and, without touching any other property, recovered the tea.

Their raid was successful. As there was an ebb tide, even the warship lying off the quay could not bring her guns to bear on the free traders, and they fastened their contraband to their saddles and rode off.

They appeared the next morning at Fordingbridge in Hampshire, and after breakfast they divided the tea among themselves. Then they proceeded through Fordingbridge, watched by crowds of inhabitants.

Among the spectators was Daniel Chater, a shoemaker, known to Diamond, alias Jack of Diamonds, one of the cavalcade of smugglers. They shook hands, and Diamond threw Chater a bag of tea.

Shortly afterwards, a royal proclamation appeared promising a reward for apprehending those persons who were concerned in breaking open the Custom House.

Diamond, suspected of being one of the wrongdoers, was taken into custody at Chichester. The Collector of Customs at Southampton, hearing that Chater knew Diamond, negotiated with him, and Chater agreed, at a price, to turn informer and identify Diamond.

Chater was sent with William Galley, a Custom House Officer, to deliver a letter to Major Battin, a Justice of the Peace living in Sussex. The two unfortunate men were entrapped by the smugglers, who had obtained information of their journey. They were dragged away, brutally beaten, and finally cruelly murdered.

This crime came to light six or seven months later by the confession of one of the murderers, who was in custody on some other charge. Fifteen smugglers were concerned in the murder, many of whom were apprehended, and a special commission was set up to try them at Chichester, the murder having been committed in the County of Sussex.

The trials lasted from the 16th to the 19th of April, 1748. Seven of the prisoners were convicted and executed.

On the 4th of April in the same year, five of the smugglers concerned in the breaking open of the Custom House at Poole were indicted at the Old Bailey for that offence, and for stealing from the Custom House thirty-seven hundredweight of tea.

Four of them were convicted, of whom one was pardoned, the three others being executed.

Kingsmill and Perin, two of those who were hanged, remained insolent to the last, maintaining that they were not guilty of robbery, for after all, it was their own tea which they had recovered.

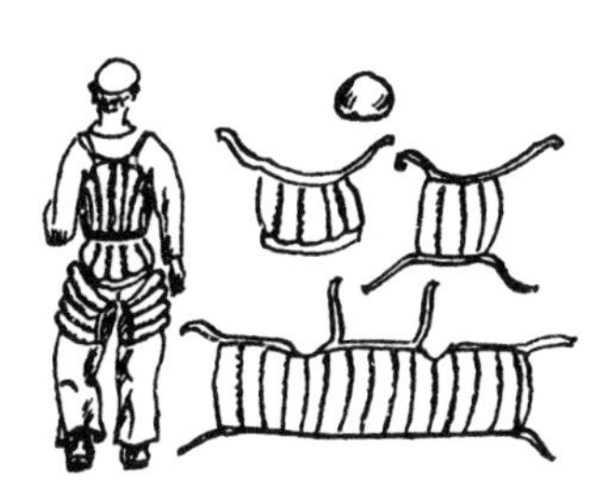

Tea smuggling

19

The Isle of Wight

THIS small, historic island — 'Vectis' of Roman times — shaped like a diamond, and about 145 square miles in area, with the Medina as its main river, was the ideal haven for the smuggler, for, situated as it is in the English Channel, and separated from the mainland by the Solent and Spithead, it made a convenient landing place for cargoes from France and the Channel Islands, and a shelter for goods en route to the Hampshire coast.

Parts of the coast were perfect for the purposes of the smuggler. Some of the easier landing places, such as Sandham, or Sandown, on the south coast of the island, with its fort of twenty guns, were under the immediate eye of authority, but the 'back of the Wight', from Rocken End to the Needles, with its wild and rugged beauty of cliffs rising sometimes four hundred feet above the sea as at Black Gang Chine and Walpen Chine, was at once ideal and dangerous for smuggling.

This coast included places such as Ladder Chine, a semicircular erosion made by the sea and the wind, and the shingle beach of Chale Bay, which stretches from St. Catherine's Point to the treacherous Atherfield Rocks.

Only the superb skill of the fishermen-smugglers could bring in a load of contraband to these lonely, dangerous shores, and it was the unhesitating bravery of these same men which saved many lives from the ships which were not infrequently wrecked on this coast.

One of these men, by the name of John Wheeler, an ex-man-o-war man turned fisherman-smuggler, one October day in 1836, with a rope tied round his waist, entered the churning sea to rescue three men from the *Clarendon* as she was pounded to destruction at the foot of Blackgang Chine.

An extraordinary feature of this wreck was that a Miss Gourlay, who perished in the wreck, was swept away by the tide, and her body was finally deposited on the shore in front of the house of her father, Captain Gourlay, R.N.

After this particular storm a lighthouse was begun at St. Catherine's Point, and finally completed in 1840.

The chief traffic of the fishermen-smugglers was in brandy from Barfleur or Cherbourg. They usually carried out their unlawful activities during the fishing season, from May to September, for during this period it did not excite much comment if the men were away for days at a time.

On their return, after favourable weather, a note or message might be left at a pre-arranged spot saying that there had been a 'good catch'. Such a message immediately resulted in the lander and his men making their way with all haste to the cliffs, where they secured the 'catch' and removed it to suitable hiding-places.

Practically all the houses on the East and West coasts of the Island were used as places of concealment. Indeed, at Atherfield or Southdown, many an old fisherman's cottage, built on the coast, was likely to have a tiny window in an attractive gable overlooking the sea, or in one end of the cottage built higher than the rest, from which a signal light could be seen only by those at sea.

Most of the cottages contained hides of various kinds. For instance, there were escape hatches to the roof through the tops of cupboards, and the removal of certain chimney bricks or bedroom floorboards would reveal a retreat beside the chimney. Refuge could also be found under the floors of outhouses, and at Rancome there was reputed to have been room enough underground to conceal a horse and cart.

When it became necessary, either through inclement weather or keen vigilance on the part of the Revenue Officers, for brandy tubs to be disposed of quickly before landing, they were often sunk in a rocky spot to avoid the sweeps, or searches at sea by the excisemen. The goods were later retrieved by means of a 'drag' or 'crocodile' made by the local smith.

Other handy instruments made by this craftsman were pumps small enough to be inserted in large jars of contraband spirit which were concealed under outhouse floors. The spirit was pumped up when required, so avoiding the necessity of digging up the jar when a customer called for his supply.

Hiding places for contraband were many and varied, and apart from concealing goods under hedgerows and covering them with sacks, cabbage patches, and even furrows in fields were planted with unusual crops.

In 1872, John Cook, a carter, ploughing in Withybed Field not far from Mottistone, laid open a furrow of great depth and width, and it remained untouched until the end of the day, but by dawn on the following day it had been 'cropped', and that particular section of the field lay fallow for a long time until it was safe to remove the contraband.

The Collector of Customs for the Isle of Wight from 1777 to 1801 was William Arnold, father of the much more famous Dr. Arnold of Rugby. William Arnold allotted beats to the Riding Officers of Excise as follows:

> "Along the north coast of the island from Cowes to Newtown Harbour; from Newtown through Yarmouth, out by the high ridge to the Needles, round by the cliffs at the back of the Island by Freshwater Gate, and along the south coast as far as Atherfield Rocks; from Atherfield Rocks along the cliffs through Chale to Crab Niton: from Crab Niton by the undercliff, through the hamlet of Shanklin and up to Sandham Fort; from thence over Culver Down, along the east coast by Bimbridge Rocks, Brading Harbour and St. Helens Roads, round through the village of Ride and across Wooton Bridge to East Cowes."

Which was quite an area to cover thoroughly.

The hazards which faced the excisemen and their helpers in the course of their duties were innumerable, and sometimes most unusual. On one occasion, a garden at Chale was being searched, an iron bar being used to prod the ground. Progress was being made towards some beehives where, in fact, brandy tubs were hidden, when suddenly, 'quite by accident', their owner upset one of the hives, and the customs officer fled from the garden.

Dogs played their part in helping the smugglers. A shepherd from Chale Abbey Farm saw a customs man hot on the heels of a friend of his who had, slung over his back, a keg containing spirits. The shepherd whistled to his dog, gave a command, and pointed at the exciseman. The dog ran off at once, and harried the unfortunate man, whilst the offender got away, and in the confusion managed to dispose of his sack and its contents.

Later, when the shepherd was questioned, the officer had to admit that he could not prove what the shepherd had shouted at the dog. The shepherd, a resourceful man, later retrieved the keg for safe keeping.

The free traders, however, did not always get away scot free, as the following episode, which occurred about 1870, shows.

Lieutenant Rattray, in charge of the Coastguard at Brook, was an alert officer. His habit was to go his rounds mounted on a white horse. Knowing this, the free traders were able to spot him in time to warn the rest of their gang of his presence in the area. It also happened that another gentleman of good standing who was friendly to the smugglers, always rode a black horse, and so that the smugglers would recognise him from a distance, he always came uphill at a gallop, and walked down to the shore.

One day, William Cook, a fisherman-smuggler, sailed off to his lobster pots off Chilton, and later brought back a haul of contraband tubs. As it was high tide, he landed them at Crab Pool, where he could be concealed from view by sailing under the straight side of the cliff. The rest of his gang, being prepared for the landing, had fixed a rope with a strong canvas sling to a stalwart post at the top of the cliff, and Cook soon had most of the tubs hauled away to the cliff top.

Meanwhile, the look-out, Reuben Cooper, saw a black horse and rider gallop uphill and proceed at walking pace down to the shore. Supposing this to be their friendly visitor, he gave no warning to the gang.

To his amazement, the 'friendly visitor' turned out to be none other than Rattray, who had changed his mount for the occasion. Although the rest of the men escaped, the astonished Cook, caught with the last few tubs in the sling, was arrested by Rattray.

He appeared before the Newport magistrates, was dispossessed of his boat and fishing tackle, and sentenced to a term of imprisonment at Winchester.

In later years, the police played their part in keeping down smuggling, and the story has been told of a gang of smugglers who left three of their number near Totland as a decoy to be arrested whilst the rest escaped with a valuable cargo.

Appearing before the Newport Bench, the Irish policeman who arrested the three men was asked by the prisoners' solicitor how he had managed to carry out such a feat singlehanded.

"Och sure", replied he, "an 'Oi surrounded them, sor!"

One of the chief difficulties which Arnold, the island Customs Officer, had to face was to employ with maximum efficiency the small water-guard allotted to him.

Ships operating in the Needles Channel were usually anchored in Yarmouth Roads waiting for suitable sailing conditions, or taking on board fresh stocks of stores and water, whilst those coming by way of Spithead anchored in St. Helen's Roads. Consequently, there were often large collections of ships lying at anchor which could engage in free-trading. To combat this, only one patrol boat of six oars was based at Yarmouth for the Needles' traffic, and the other was based at St. Helen's.

The 'sitters', or coxwains of these boats were men of daring and enterprise. During 1789, when the Revenue Cutter was away refitting, a sitter by the name of Richie petitioned Mr. Arnold for the use of a lugger, saying that if he were allowed the use of a 26-ton seized lugger then lying at Cowes, he would be able to cruise in the smugglers' tracks with much greater probability of success than he could in his open boat "in the present unsettled weather".

Arnold readily agreed to this suggestion, and reported later that although Richie had barely cruised a week in the lugger, he had, "sent in a boat with 116 casks of spirits, which is proof that the smugglers are availing themselves of the cutter's absence by carrying on a brisk trade".

In 1784, Pitt, determined to put down smuggling by all possible means, introduced the 'Hovering Act', and, by this Act, "any vessel found hovering within three miles of the coast, having aboard spirits in casks smaller than sixty gallons, and every vessel of sixty tons or under carrying any wines, tea or coffee, was to be forfeited".

Fines of £500 were to be paid by the masters of smuggling vessels who concealed their true identity by flying pennants used by the Admiralty or Customs.

According to Mr. Keble Chatterton, under the conditions of a chase, a rule of 1807 for Revenue Officers stated, "before firing on a smuggler, the cruiser was bound to hoist his Revenue Colours — both pennant and ensign — no matter whether day or night".

One of the many running sea fights took place off the Isle of Wight in August of 1784, when two of His Majesty's Revenue Cutters, *Expedition* and *Hebe* were patrolling areas along the south coast on the lookout for smugglers.

The wind was north-easterly and blowing hard when two smugglers — one a 32-gun cutter, the other a 12-gun lugger — were sighted by *Expedition* off Freshwater making for landing grounds in Christchurch Bay or Mudeford Haven.

The *Expedition* fully realised the hazards of attacking the smugglers single-handed, for it was not unknown for revenue ships to be captured by the smugglers, officers and men being kept below decks or dropped overboard, so the commander of *Expedition* contacted *Hebe* at Spithead, and both vessels took up position at the east end of the island.

Meanwhile, the wind being against them, the smugglers could not easily land their cargo, and they made off towards St. Catherine's Point, where they were sighted by the Revenue cruisers who, after hoisting their colours, fired warning shots and gave chase to the smugglers as they went about to the westwards.

For several hours a running fight continued westwards, well into the Channel. During the heat of the chase, *Expedition* had the misfortune to lose her topmast, and left the *Hebe* to carry on the fight. Towards nightfall, the smuggling cutter signalled for a cease fire to the commander of *Hebe,* giving the impression that they wished to surrender. As *Hebe* lowered her boats to go aboard the free traders' vessel, the unscrupulous offenders crowded on all sail and escaped into the night.

A report on this episode in the Hampshire Chronicle of 1784 stated:

> "This will be a caution to all King's ships never to cease their fire upon smugglers until they lower their sails. This cutter had on board 75 tons of tea and a great quantity of brandy, and had been expected for ten days past."

It is interesting to read in Arnold-Forster's book, *At War with the Smugglers,* that about 1786 a Lieutenant Crooke, Commander of H.M. Cutter *Expedition,* was court martialled at Portsmouth and dismissed his ship on a charge of smuggling. The cutter had on board "Forty small casks of spirits, twenty-five bottles of Portugal, 347 bottles of French wine; an excessive amount for the use of so small a vessel — even though a man-of-war!"

20

Dorset

POOLE Harbour, into which pour the rivers Frome and Trent or Piddle, with its unfrequented foreshore extending for one hundred miles, provided splendid opportunities for the smugglers to land their cargoes. Once they were past the Preventive Station on Brownsea Island at the entrance to the harbour they were away with all speed to get their goods to markets at Wareham and Wimborne, and even further afield to Sturminster Newton, Stalbridge and Shaftesbury.

From Poole Harbour to the West are the rising hills of the Isle of Purbeck. This lovely part of Dorset, with splendid cliffs sheltering curving sea-water bays, and the rugged and rocky coast with its quarries and secret caves, was a perfect landing ground for contraband at the end of a run.

The lonely downland with its wild and solitary valleys leading inland to secret passages or hiding places in the hills, and the grey stone cottages which boasted vaulted cellars or trapdoors in their roofs, made the disposal of cargo relatively easy.

Studland Bay, its golden sandy shores sweeping round to Handfast point with the dazzling white stacks of 'Old Harry and his Wife' was an open invitation for easy landings. From such thatched cottages as 'Smugglers' Watch' built high on the rising hills overlooking the bay, the lookout could see any activities of the customs officers and warn the smugglers if their landings were endangered.

The sweep of bare Ballard Down rolling towards the coast at the white cliff's edge, where the seagulls wheel and cry, and the curve of Swanage Bay, made an extensive smuggling ground — but Parson's Barn, a cave near the Old Harry Rocks, was a particular favourite in which to store tobacco or brandy.

The reef of low rocks which ran out to the sea off Peveril Point was dangerous to sailors, but beyond, the magnificent cliff forming Durlston Head rising from Durlston Bay must have been a hive of illicit industry. There were stoneyards from which the boats took their loads of stone at a roughly made quay, and the 'Tilly Whim Caves' left by the quarried stone were superb for the smugglers' use, although they could only be reached in safety during calm weather.

From Dancing Ledge to St. Aldhelm's Head, where the rugged cliffs rise some 410 feet above the sea, the rocky coast continues towards the hidden beauty of Chapman's Pool, and the strange blackness of the shale of Kimmeridge Bay.

Further westwards, charming Lulworth Cove, almost encircled by soaring cliffs, leads to the unexpected fascination of Durdle Door, where strata millions of years old meet on the rocky arch.

Ringstead Bay with its road rising steeply to the hinterland is close to the soft sea-washed sands of Weymouth Bay and the grim shores of Portland Isle.

From the 'island' is the magnificent panorama of the sea-fringed shingle bank of the Chesil Beach sweeping to West Bay where Bridport Harbour fights continually to keep its small jetty strong against the buffeting seas. Beyond Golden Cap is the charming old sea-town of Lyme Regis.

There was hardly any part of the Dorset Coast which was not used by the free-traders and where cargoes from France were not landed.

* * * *

"SPIRITS FROM THE VASTY DEEP"

The market boat was on its way from Swanage to Poole one sunny day, and two strangers, who were passengers, were gazing into the calm water beneath them; as they passed Parson's Barn, the smugglers' cave, they saw some floating pieces of cork.

"What are these things?" they asked.

"Why, they be markers to show where the lobster pots do lie", answered one of the boatmen.

"We've never seen lobster pots before; do you think we could have a look at some?" queried one of the strangers.

"Well — Oi don't rightly know if t'would be the thing to do, sort of pullin 'em up now, might be difficult".

"That'll be all right", said another boatman, "I don't reckon they markers 'ave been there long".

So up they pulled the lobster pots — and tubs.

"We'd better drop those back, quick like", said a boatman, lowering the contraband quickly into the water.

"Stop a moment", cried one of the strangers, "a little in my line, I think", and he instructed the boatmen to raise the tubs on to the deck. He then took a blade and marked the tubs with arrows, and ordered, "Right, now drop them overboard".

The smugglers were caught when they came 'lobster-fishing' and were astonished to see the markings on the tubs. One of the strangers on board the market boat had been the new Customs Officer for Swanage!

Mr. W. M. Hardy, an authority on smuggling in the Purbecks, said that on taking down a stone merchant's house in Dorset he found a little nook in which were "6 pewter canisters of good scented snuff". In the thick stone walls of the local houses many openings which were used as hiding places were covered with wallpaper and usually over that was hung the family picture.

As a young man Mr. Hardy came into contact with the secretary and manager of a smugglers' gang. He said that although they had operated for a long time very successfully, they did have a run of ill luck, and about the year 1840 the free-traders had the misfortune to lose three cargoes at Lytchett, Swanage Bay and Durlston Bay.

About this time, of course, the coastguards had been reinforced and their vigilance had been well rewarded. These heavy losses discouraged this particular gang, with the result that they stopped smuggling on a large scale at Swanage.

An extraordinary tale is told about a violent storm of 1823, when a sloop, the *Ebenezer,* was blown ashore and lifted to the top of Chesil Bank. When the storm blew over it is reported that the vessel was "launched again on the East side of the beach", and thus became known as the "only vessel which ever came up the English Channel without going round Portland Bill".

During this storm, Mr. Hardy's grandfather, then a boy, was in the *Purveyor,* a ship moored in ballast with two anchors down in South Deep.

The only men on board during the height of the storm were the mate, Phineas Harden and the boy, Peter Haysome. Unfortunately both the anchor chains parted and the ship, with the helpless sailors on board, was driven towards Parkstone. The mate 'instead of imitating the Bible Phineas and holding up his hands in supplication, went down on his knees and asked for aid and mercy'.

The result of the supplication or, more especially the unusually high tide, was that they were left in a field of turnips — high and dry. There were hardly any houses in Parkstone or Bournemouth in those days.

When the gale died down, the ship's owner, who came

from Swanage, had to employ men to dig a channel from the vessel to the sea so that she could be refloated.

During this long operation, the captain visited the ship several times, and one day he thought he would inspect the hold. When he removed the hatches he found a load of tubs!

He immediately informed the Custom House Officer at Poole, and for this he was given £50 reward, which covered the cost of getting the ship refloated. Not only had the captain been in danger of losing his ship at sea, but also on land. No doubt the labourers were smugglers, and great opportunists!

* * * *

"UP ALONG AND DOWN ALONG"

Many and varied were the hiding places which the gentlemen used, but none could have been more dramatic than the 'Shillibier' which was a grand miniature catafalque borne on a four wheeled hearse.

This formidable and sepulchural contraption was devised by a Mr. Shillibeer for use at important funerals of the Georgian and Victorian era.

The vehicle, which was so large that both the body and the pall bearers could be comfortably transported, was shrouded in black crepe, and even the wheels had black cloth coverings; enormous black plumes topped the black wooden pedestals and gave height to the already large conveyance.

An innkeeper of Poole owned both a livery stable and a Shillibier, together with funeral coaches and splendid black horses. These he would hire to the undertakers for funerals, and, without any qualms at all, he hired them out to the smugglers for transporting contraband to Wimborne or Ringwood.

The Preventive men do not appear to have suspected this method of conveying these earthly goods from one town to another. It may be that they never saw the midnight drive of the awe-inspiring cortège, with the Shillibier, plumes and drapery flying, drawn by fine black horses and galloping over the heath or down the country lanes until it approached a village or town, when it proceeded with stately decorum.

For years the free traders used the Shillibier and they were never discovered to be carrying contraband.

* * * *

A smuggler of Upton called Bennet lived at a turnpike gate situated on the main Hamworthy Road. He and his gang were reputed to have kept boats in Lytchett Bay from whence they sailed past Brownsea Island to Sandbanks and then made out to sea where they had a rendezvous with a smuggling lugger.

They returned to Upton to hide their contraband in an underground cave until it was safe to load the kegs into a waggon sent by a merchant from Salisbury.

* * * *

The Ark, an old French smuggling lugger which had been drawn up on the beach at Wyke Regis, used to be the living quarters of the Preventive Men. Their duties were carried out chiefly at Ferry Bridge, which was formerly known as the 'Passage'. An old print shows a ferry crossing there in 1790.

These Preventive Men were "armed with cutlass and pistol and carried a small rocket which had a blue light and which they fired if they heard a boat rowing".

* * * *

The men of Portland were reported to have smuggled small kegs of brandy under their top hats when dressed in their Sunday best.

* * * *

It was not unusual for the smugglers to 'haunt' the churchyards, and at Winterbourne Monkton they 'dressed up images' to intimidate the customs men.

* * * *

There was, until 1912, a coastguard station in the hamlet of Seatown to the west of Bridport Harbour. The old people of the area have said that some old smugglers' cottages fell into the sea due to the slipping away of the coast. The fishermen-smugglers who lived there were 'a hardy lot' they say.

*   *   *   *

From West Bay, the chief route of the free-traders would appear to have been "through Powerstock and Hooke, then over Toller Down". At Toller Down there was an inn much frequented by the smugglers called *The Jolly Sailor*. The ruins of the inn may still be there.

For a considerable time a successful gang of free-traders, under the leadership of a man called the 'Colonel' operated along the coast from Seatown to Charmouth. Their chief landing ground was St. Gabriel's Mouth. Much of the contraband was delivered locally and the Church Tower was used as a hiding place in an emergency, but the free traders usually worked their way across Marshwood Vale to inland market towns.

*   *   *   *

Further inland, at Corscombe, it has been said that there is, near Court Farm, a cottage by the name of Woodwalls where there was once a school.

Tradition has it that boys at the school used to help to dig large vaults which were for the sole purpose of concealing contraband. In fact, a nephew of one of these boys remembered his uncle telling him how he used to wheel away barrow-loads of earth!

* * * *

Many old inhabitants of Halstock Leigh speak of a pond at Daisy Farm which is believed to be paved so that any kegs which were hidden there could be removed without much trouble. Apparently there were also vaults at Pear Tree Farm which were used for concealing contraband.

According to tradition, an old pack horse route, which is now a bridle path by the name of Pen Lane, runs from Halstock Mill to Pendomer. At this point the route went into Somerset, where, at Hartington there was another secret vault.

So the journeying tubs travelled over hills and through valleys many miles inland from their landing place on the coast until they came to rest in some quiet country village or market town.

* * * *

In 1734, at Kingston, Mr. John Pitt bought Encomb, the old Eldon Home, which he rebuilt in Purbeck Stone. In order to discourage the local people from smuggling he set up a local twine spinning industry for the manufacture of sacking cordage and sailcloth. How far he was successful in preventing smuggling can only be a matter of conjecture, for the spirit of adventure was strong in these people.

Lulworth also had its complement of venturers and caves for storing their contraband. Generally they had very successful runs of cargo, but, occasionally they were obstructed by young and fearless Riding Officers.

On one occasion a young officer was captured when he was on his rounds and the smugglers told him in no uncertain terms to stop spying on them or they would "marke him as he should be known thereby, for he was one as did dyscover ther doings". Another, not so lucky, was pushed over the cliff. For this dastardly deed three men were arrested and condemned to long imprisonment.

Dogs were used to help the men in Lulworth, and strong swimming animals were taught to bring in logs of wood from the sea. When they were proficient at this the dogs were promoted to swimming in with ropes of kegs attached to the logs and they delivered the goods to their masters.

Contraband from Lulworth was usually sent to the market at Sturminster Newton. The main depot for these goods was Fiddleford Farm. The leader of the packhorses which brought in the kegs was one which belonged to Roger Ridout, and it was known as 'Ridout's stumpted tail'.

The following extracts from a diary of William Money, an officer on leave from his work with the Navy of the Honourable East India Company, give a first hand report on events at Lulworth in 1798: —

> "Sept. 4th, 1798. At Lulworth Cove. When we returned to dinner we found a serious quarrel in progress between the

landlord and some smugglers. Espied in a little sandy bay a gang of smugglers carousing in their cave, their vessel being hauled up on the beach.

Sept. 6th. Saw a cutter working for Lulworth Cove, it proved to be a smuggler from Alderney who landed a cargo in the night."

Another story from West Lulworth, told by the Misses J. and P. Loader is one which happened before the Battle of Trafalgar when the whole of the South coast was alert to the dangers of invasion by the French.

A certain smuggler-farmer, believed to have lived at St. Andrew's Farm was married to a china manufacturer's daughter who had learned to speak French in order to help her father when dealing with the Sèvres pottery's traders who bought china clay, and also sold their goods in England.

One night, she knew that one of the local landowners who had a vested interest in a valuable cargo which was being run, was giving a special dinner party for the Riding Officers and their men, and she also knew that the press gang were out in force. Worried about her father's safety she ran down the hill leading to the Cove.

There she saw a strange looking ship which appeared to her to be a Revenue Cutter, and, hiding behind some rocks, she heard a boat grating on the shingle. Two men disembarked, leaving the sailors in the boat. To her astonishment one of the men looked like Napoleon, and she heard him discussing the possibilities of landing an invasion fleet at that point on the coast.

By lantern light they studied a map. Then Napoleon faced

with the difficulties of negotiating and landing on the Dorset coast, with a shrug, refolded his map and said, regretfully, "Impossible". He turned away from his companion and re-joined his vessel anchored off the entrance to the Cove.

The farmer's wife who told this story was born in 1784 and lived to be 104 years old.

* * * *

Smugglers' Haunt is the name given to an inn at Trickett's Cross on the main road from London to the West Country. The inn has been rebuilt on approximately the same spot as an old smugglers' rendezvous. Once a solitary building in the lone hinterland, it provided a rest and sanctuary for the tired free-trader who had walked or ridden inland through the long night.

* * * *

The most respectable and able parishioners of Kingston, Warmwell, Woodsford and Tincleton turned occasionally to smuggling as an additional income.

Many times have the cliffs of Ringstead Bay or Whitenose witnessed a gathering of these villagers who, after a day in the fields, had walked eight or nine miles to unload cargoes of brandy from the small boats on the shore.

Then back home they marched, carrying their kegs, until the dawn, when they returned to a day's work as if they had enjoyed a good night's sleep!

Certainly they had contact with the 'Government folk', as they called the Preventive Officers, but this was only at infrequent intervals.

When George Treviss, a smuggler, was asked if he had ever cut about and killed any Government folk, he replied that he had not, but that he had helped to tie 'em to a post often!

"Twixt the Lizard and Dover
We hand the stuff over,
Though I may not inform how we do it, and when
But a light on each quarter
Low down on the water
Is well understood by poor honest men!"

Poor Honest Men,
by Rudyard Kipling.

21

Devon

MEN of Devon have a proud heritage; their valiant countrymen have fought for England's honour and their inheritance is one of supreme scenic beauty.

There are green hills veined with the red earth of Devon, swift-flowing streams and brown-stained rivers from the moorland sparkling down the deep luxuriant valleys, sometimes wandering through well-wooded and lush meadowland or sweeping along to historic harbours where great ships have sheltered and from whence great fleets have sailed.

The secluded bays, pale purple-pink pebbled beaches, narrow coves and craggy cliffs with steep and broken paths were known to fishermen of long ago.

Places like Seaton and Beer had their fishermen-smugglers, and doubtless they found adventurous excitement in hoodwinking the excisemen, as well as bringing in extra money for their families from the contraband they brought ashore.

Sidmouth, Exeter, Branscombe, Holcombe, Teignmouth, Plymouth, Lynmouth, Martinhoe, Ilfracombe and Barnstaple, together with many more such names, were all linked with the romantic and wild days of smuggling.

There remain today examples of the 'Smuggler's Sign' which consisted of the ends of glass bottles built into a wall usually under the eaves of cottages and houses, to show that a discreet and friendly welcome awaited the smugglers.

Captain J. R. W. Coxhead writes that some of these bottle-ends can be seen at a cottage on the main Axminster-Honiton road, and even Wilmington School House has the signs embedded in a gable-end.

A sunken lane in Seaton, a hidden shaft about 12 feet down in a field for hiding contraband, and an altar tomb in Branscombe churchyard to the memory of Custom House Officer, John Hurley, killed during the course of his duty, all bear witness to the smuggling which was prevalent throughout Devon.

22

Jack Rattenbury

A FAMOUS smuggler hero of Devon was Jack Rattenbury or 'The Rob Roy of the West' as he was called on an old print which used to hang in the Anchor Hotel at Beer.

Before Jack Rattenbury was born in 1778, his father, a village shoemaker at Beer, was believed to have been press-ganged to a man-o'-war. His mother, an independent and hardy woman, was left to make a living by marketing fish. His uncle was a fisherman and Jack went with him to sea at the age of nine.

During one fishing expedition he accidentally lost the boat's rudder and his uncle severely whipped him with a rope's end, so he then left his family to become an apprentice to a Brixham fisherman. Unfortunately during his apprenticeship he was severely bullied by his older workmates and so he returned to Beer where his uncle was getting together a crew for his vessel which he proposed to use as a privateer.

Jack re-joined his uncle. By the time he was sixteen he had been captured by an armed Frenchman, escaped to America and returned to Beer by way of Le Havre and Guernsey.

After all this excitement he found ordinary fishing a tedious livelihood and so joined a vessel smuggling cognac from the Channel Islands to Lyme Regis. His next ship was *The Friends* of Bridport. This vessel, honestly engaged in proceeding to Tenby for culm, was unfortunately intercepted and taken by a French Privateer on Jack's very first voyage in her.

When the privateer was off Swanage, he cleverly escaped and swam to the shore, where he contacted a Revenue Cutter, *The Nancy*. She overhauled *The Friends*, recaptured her and took her into Cowes.

Rattenbury, once more restored to *The Friends*, hadn't been on board for more than two days when he was press-ganged into the Navy. After a fortnight of this enforced duty he again escaped. This time he joined an expedition to Newfoundland bent on fishing for cod. Again his luck was out, for a Spanish Privateer took over the fishing vessel and took it to Vigo. With his usual skill, he managed to escape again and returned to Beer where has was married to a beautiful local girl on the 17th April, 1801. He went to live at Lyme Regis. His career then moved from privateering on the Coast of West Africa to piloting vessels. During his latter activities he was impressed once more, only to escape again.

Returning to Beer he took up fishing. During his expeditions he collected contraband from the lonely shores of Dorset and Hampshire and brought the goods back to Beer.

One of the smugglers' store-houses was at Christchurch, Hampshire, where he and his gang unloaded vast quantities of contraband.

On one occasion, off the shores, the *Roebuck* Revenue

Cutter captured his vessel and impounded his load of gin. Rattenbury, with customary daring, not only hid in the bottom of the cutter's boat and escaped when it arrived on shore, but also had the nerve to set free his own men and get away with three kegs of gin.

Many of Jack Rattenbury's escapes are told in his own words in *Memoirs of a Smuggler.* He would appear to have lost many cargoes in his time, but he always survived capture to carry on smuggling again.

The Revenue Officers patrolling the English Channel were extremely vigilant and watched the coast with eagle eyes. After one smuggling run Jack was mortified to have his goods confiscated by these 'indefatigable pickaroons'.

One of these officers, a lieutenant from the *Greyhound,* found out that Jack was in Weymouth and pursued him. Taking evasive action Rattenbury hid in a public house where he knew the landlord well. In the early hours of the morning, however, the lieutenant awakened the publican, threatening to fire at the landlord through the window and force his way in if he did not allow him to enter the inn.

Rattenbury immediately climbed up a chimney and stayed there for almost an hour, barely able to breathe in such a confined space. Meanwhile the officer searched the inn but did not find his quarry. After the lieutenant had gone, down came the smuggler, bruised and covered in soot but triumphant at having escaped from the officer.

The Spring of 1806 was foggy when Rattenbury had the misfortune to be captured by the revenue cutter the *Duke of*

York, as he was returning with a consignment of contraband tubs from Alderney.

He and his men were removed to Dartmouth where they were fined £100, given the choice of serving in a man-o-war or being sent to gaol. After being a short time in gaol they decided to serve in one of His Majesty's Ships. They were transferred to a brig in Dartmouth Roads.

Rattenbury chose his time carefully and escaped from a navy tender by jumping into an approaching fishing boat whilst the officers-in-charge were intoxicated. He was put ashore at Kings Wear after which he ran for a mile, rode a borrowed horse to Brixham and from there sailed a hired fishing-boat to Beer.

He turned up again to buy a share in a smuggling galley. This vessel foundered and Rattenbury and a companion were rowing in an open boat when they fell in with a man-o'-war and were taken prisoner. After a trial at Falmouth they were sentenced to imprisonment in Bodmin Gaol.

For the journey from Falmouth to Bodmin they were put into the charge of two thirsty constables, who stopped at every inn on the way. By the evening they had reached a solitary inn called the *Indian Queen*, and Rattenbury and his companion had planned an escape. They refused to obey the constables' orders to enter the post-chaise, and after struggling with the officers — during which time Rattenbury missed being shot by inches — they cleared off over the moors and joined some smugglers who sheltered them at Newquay for the night.

On the following day they rode to Mevagissey, sailed to Budleigh Salterton and eventually walked home again to Beer.

From time to time Rattenbury was either captured or on the point of being arrested for deserting His Majesty's Navy. One other incident occurred at the end of three profitable smuggling trips to Alderney.

Thinking it was safe to do so, Jack went ashore with his friends for a drink in one of the local Devonshire inns. He soon realized that he was in a roomful of the South Devon Militia.

A sergeant, realizing that Jack Rattenbury was amongst them, made his way towards him and said,

"You are my prisoner. You are a deserter, and must go along with me".

Jack coolly replied:

"Sergeant, you are surely labouring under an error, I have done nothing that can authorize you in taking me up, or detaining me; you must certainly have mistaken me for some other person".

The rest of the soldiers had, by now, arms and muskets but Rattenbury calmly continued to talk to the sergeant, and, as he did so, he rapidly jumped into the cellar and took off his jacket and shirt so none could hold him.

Arming himself with a reaphook he then defied the soldiers to arrest him saying he would kill the first man who came near him, adding that he himself would not leave that spot alive. The terrified sergeant bellowed at his men "Soldiers, do your duty, seize him". Their reply was:

"Sergeant, you proposed it; take the lead, and set us an example, and we will follow".

The extraordinary thing was that for four hours Rattenbury held off the soldiers, and finally the sergeant sent a message for help to Lieutenant Durall.

Suddenly the tension was broken by some resourceful women from Beer who dashed into the inn and created a diversion by shrieking, "There's been a shipwreck and a boy lies drowning — come and help him — quickly". Seizing his opportunity Rattenbury hurled himself through the crowd, tore down to the beach, boarded his vessel and straightaway flew his colours.

Jack later tried to give up his smuggling ways and decided to take over a public house, but somehow fortune seemed to be against him, and either that or a natural inclination drove him back to free-trading.

In 1812, soon after he had gone to sea again, he was chased by a cruiser which had been standing off Torbay and whose prime purpose was the protection of the fishing fleet off Brixham. On boarding Jack's vessel all that the irate commander could find was a bottle containing a pint of gin. The indignant Jack protested:

"You have treated us shamefully. You have taken my vessel on the high seas and retained it, though you found nothing on board to justify you on being so; and it is, I conceive, an act of piracy".

The Commander replied, "I care nothing about it".

On hearing what had happened, Jack's wife came aboard and he quickly told her to procure a boat and come for him the next morning.

When she arrived with some companions on the next day, only the second mate was in charge of the vessel for the rest of the officers were on shore. This was ideal for Jack's plan.

As soon as his wife was alongside Rattenbury jumped into the boat and signalled to his companions to join him — ostensibly to help the women to board the cruiser. His gang jumped into the small boat and, after the women had climbed on board the cruiser he shouted, "Shove off", and pushed an oar against its side. The second mate grabbed at the oar, breaking the blade. Angrily Jack hurled the rest of the oar at the mate and shouted to his gang, "Hoist the sail". The mate roared, "If you do, I'll fire at you! "

"Make sure of your mark then", shouted the smuggler.

The resulting shot tore through the little boat's sails.

As the mate re-loaded, Rattenbury's wife, now on board the cruiser, grabbed the pistol from his hands, but on recovering it, he took aim again and the shot struck the sail-rope, and the sail collapsed.

The mate then stopped firing, thinking that Rattenbury and his men would return on board; but, during this respite the smugglers hoisted sail once more and were off.

The navy lowered a boat and pursued them, peppering their sails with shot, but, fortunately injuring no one. Steering the boat to Hope's Nose, Rattenbury followed his companions as they left the boat and made for the shore. He was narrowly missed by a shot which was fired perilously close to his head.

Once on shore he scrambled up the cliffs, and on reaching the top, glanced back but he did not see anybody. He took off his jacket and dropped it in the hope that it would mislead his pursuers. He then rolled down the cliffs to a spot close to his original landing place.

Several hundred people had by now gathered on Brixham Cliffs and were watching the rest of Jack's gang being chased by the navy. Lying hidden for a long time, he eventually saw the sailors return to their boat and push off to the cruiser. When it was safe to do so Rattenbury made his way over hedges, fields and ditches and finally reached Torquay in safety. Two of the fugitives were later captured and put on a sloop-o'-war and set sail for the West Indies.

Rattenbury reached home safely and his wife joined him later.

The closure of his inn during 1813, and the strict measures taken by the navy in the channel, which made smuggling very difficult, gave Rattenbury a hard time. Although he piloted a few vessels and fished a little he earned scarcely enough to keep his wife and four children.

He did make a profitable trip to Cherbourg in 1814, but he had another unlucky spell during which a gale ruined one run. Another time his boats were seized by a revenue cruiser and then a custom house vessel sailed over a marker buoy and a hundred or more kegs were discovered on the sea bed.

Rattenbury continued smuggling and he had several more

years of success coupled with the inevitable failure or capture and narrow escape. His memoirs reveal some of the funnier moments in his free-trading experiences.

He wrote:

> "On one occasion I had a goose on board which the master who overhauled the vessel was very desirous of buying; but I was too well aware of the value of the stuffing to part with it, for instead of onions and sage, it consisted of fine lace."

He related another experience which did not end too happily for him:

> "Having landed a cargo at Seaton Hole one dark night, I was going up the cliff with a keg at my back, when I had the ill-luck to stumble over an ass, which began to bray so horribly that together with the noise occasioned by my fall, woke an officer who was taking a nap below, in consequence of which he seized nearly forty kegs, being the whole of the cargo."

This swarthy free-trader endured the tough and dangerous life which he led with a tremendous zest and gaiety. It was only at the latter part of 1825 that he had a severe set back when he was taken prisoner as he was approaching Dawlish on his return from a run.

He was held prisoner for almost a month in the watch house at Budleigh Salterton before being brought to Exeter. Here he was sent to gaol for two years.

Then Lord Teignmouth reported that in 1829 Rattenbury made an application to Lord Rolle who gave him a letter to the Admiral at Portsmouth, and he went aboard the *Tartar* cutter. In January 1830 he took his discharge, received his pay at the custom house, and went home.

He reverted to smuggling interspersed with attempts at honest trading, but bad luck dogged him, and a custom house boat from Beer caught him after he had dropped his cargo overboard, and, although all that could be found was a fathom's length of rope, Jack Rattenbury together with his eldest son and two others of his gang were tried at Lyme Regis, pronounced guilty and sent to Dorchester Gaol for another two years until 1833.

Irrepressible at 57, this man carried out his last smuggling sortie in 1836.

One night he and a companion had a cartload of brandy tubs to carry overland, but just before they reached Newton Abbot they were halted by patrolling Riding Officers who confiscated the goods. The elusive Rattenbury sped into the night, but his partner was caught.

Jack Rattenbury stopped smuggling, but his son carried on, although the days of great gains in the trade had gone.

One of the last glimpses of Jack was when he was giving evidence at Exeter Assizes in March 1836 where his son was on trial for assaulting a customs officer at Budleigh Salterton.

His son and witnesses maintained that he had been at Beer at the time of the assault.

When cross-examined by Mr. Sergeant Bompas, Jack Rattenbury said that he had reared his son properly and "Larnt him the Creed, the Lord's Prayer and Ten Commandments".

"You don't find there, 'Thou shalt not smuggle'?" queried

Mr. Sergeant Bompas. "No", was Rattenbury's prompt reply, "but I find there 'Thou shalt not bear false witness against thy neighbour'."

Fortunately the young Rattenbury avoided transportation for life by the many petitions which were received by Lord John Russell and he was granted the Royal Pardon.

The stormy adventurous and daring life of Jack Rattenbury presumably ended at Beer. Here amongst the thatched cottages and by the quiet unfrequented bay Jack could peacefully spend his time talking to the old fishermen, who knew him in the "good old smugglin' days", and he would, no doubt, be duly grateful to his benefactor, the Right Honourable Lord Rolle, who allowed him the sum of one shilling a week for the rest of his life.

23

Cruel Coppinger

AN old Cornish song tells of Cruel Coppinger, a strange and mysterious character, " a man of foreign kind", who came to the shores of Cornwall "by the salt water" and left them "carried away by the wind".

Many tales of smuggler Coppinger, the Dane, have been told by Cornishmen in the warmth of an old inn over their pints of beer or cider.

"Time was", they would say, after he disappeared, "when none durst say his name, for fear he'd come back again".

* * * *

All day the gales had pounded the northern coasts of Cornwall and by nightfall they had reached a howling crescendo..

Perched among the rocks like vultures, the wreckers awaited the end of the ship which they could see occasionally through the murk and the flying spindrift. With masts gone, and decks constantly swept by the giant waves, she headed inevitably for the cruel rocks.

Struggling with the wheel, and shouting rage and defiance at the wind and the waves was a massive figure of a man. He clung there until the very last moment, and as the rocks tore into the vessel, he hurled himself, roaring, into the sea, and with superhuman strength fought through the waves and dragged himself to the safety of the shore.

It was not the way of the wreckers to help those whom the sea had spared. Silently they watched as the man heaved his great body from the sand, surveyed the motionless crowd, and then boldly seized an old woman's scarlet cloak and flung it over his naked, dripping body.

Among the fascinated onlookers, a little apart, mounted on a white horse, was Dinah Hamlyn, a farmer's daughter. The stranger, appraising the girl and the horse, strode towards them, and with a roar flung himself on the horse's back behind the rider, whereupon the startled animal leaped forward and galloped wildly to the farm.

Dismounting, he threw open the farmhouse door and strode inside, boldly proclaiming to the astonished Hamlyns in a foreign accent that he was Daniel Coppinger, and that he came from Denmark. With these words he fell to the floor, exhausted.

Overawed by the invasion, the Hamlyns dragged their uninvited guest upstairs to bed and left him to sleep.

At breakfast the next morning the family were mildly

startled to see Coppinger, wearing Hamlyn's clothing, take the place normally reserved for the master of the house. Apparently Hamlyn was quite unconcerned, and treated it all as a joke, allowing the stranger to eat a huge breakfast.

Daniel Coppinger, persuasive of tongue and willing to work hard, stayed on at the farm. He charmed Dinah into marriage, and when her father died, took control of the farm and the family's wealth — all, that is, except Mrs. Hamlyn's own savings, which she carefully concealed from her son-in-law.

Shortly after the old farmer's death, Coppinger changed. He began to spend his new wealth, and entered on a period of wild and reckless living, caring neither for his wife's nor her mother's happiness, and treating them both with the utmost contempt.

Soon his money was spent, and he began to look round for another source of easy wealth. He gathered together a gang of unscrupulous companions, and with them he intimidated the whole of the countryside.

They turned to smuggling, and their rendezvous was at Steeple Brink, a cliff close to his farm, several hundred feet above the shore. At the foot of the cliff was a cave, reached only by way of a strong rope ladder from the cliff-top, or by boat. Much of the smugglers' cargo was landed here.

He would stop at nothing to gain his ends, and he became known for miles around as 'Cruel Coppinger'. He acquired a vessel, the *Black Prince*, which came to be feared even by the Revenue Cutters, for he mercilessly attacked any kind of ship.

One story tells of a revenue cutter commanded by an officer determined to capture Coppinger. He found the *Black Prince* and pursued her, expecting her to put up a fight, for which he was well prepared. Instead the vessel turned away. The revenue cutter gave chase, and followed *Black Prince* as she made towards a point called Gull Rock. The smugglers' ship sailed confidently through the difficult and dangerous channel to the Rock, but the cutter, following at great speed, missed the channel and splintered on the rocks. Not a man was saved.

At home, Coppinger could not be satisfied until he had laid hands on all the Hamlyn money. He had discovered by devious means that Mrs. Hamlyn still had plenty hidden away, and he relentlessly persecuted her in order to make her reveal the hiding place, but she refused.

Infuriated, Coppinger roped Dinah to a bed-post in front of her mother and, brandishing a cat-o'-nine-tails, threatened to thrash the terrified girl unless he was told where the money lay hidden. Mrs. Hamlyn could hold out no longer, and she gave him her savings.

He did use the whip though — but on a local priest, who called to rebuke him for his behaviour towards his family.

The fear and dread which the Dane spread in the hearts of the people of North Cornwall came to an end on another night of raging storm and darkness. Coppinger was last seen in the *Black Prince* near Gull Rock. The vessel headed out into the storm, and neither he nor his ship were seen again.

There is very little information to establish the identity of the real Coppinger but, according to Lord Teignmouth and Charles G. Harper in their book "The Smugglers",

"Daniel Herbert Copinger, or Coppinger, was wrecked at Welcombe Mouth on December 23rd, 1792, and was given shelter beneath the roof of Mr. William Arthur, yeoman farmer, at Golden Park, Hartland, where for many years afterwards his name might have been seen, scratched on a window pane:

> D. H. Coppinger, shipwrecked December 23 1792, kindly received by Mr. Wm. Arthur.

There is not the slightest authority for the story of his sensational leap on to the saddle of Miss Dinah Hamlyn; but it is true enough that the next year he married a Miss Hamlyn—her Christian name was Ann—elder of the two daughters of Ackland Hamlyn, of Galsham, in Hartland, and in the registers of Hartland Church may be found this entry: "Daniel Herbert Coppinger, of the King's Royal Navy, and Ann Hamlyn mard. (by licence) 3 Aug." The "damsel" of the story also turns out, by the cool calm evidence of this entry, to have been the mature age of forty two.

Mrs. Hamlyn, Coppinger's mother-in-law, died in 1800, and was buried in the Chancel of Hartland Church . . . Little else is known of Coppinger and nothing whatever of his alleged connection with the Navy. He became bankrupt in 1802, and was then a prisoner in the King's Bench Prison . . . Nothing is known of him after this date, but rumour told how he was living apart from his wife, at Barnstaple and subsisting on an allowance from her.

Mrs. Coppinger herself in after years, resided at Barnstaple and died there on Aug. 31st, 1833. She lies buried in the chancel of Hartland Church beside her mother."

24

Further Afield

IT would be a mistake to think that smuggling took place only on the South Coast of England, for Custom House records have been kept which show that this illicit trade has prevailed all round the coasts of the British Isles.

Llandudno in North Wales has had its free-traders, and a cave on Great Orme called Pigeon's Cave is reputed to have been an old smugglers' cave.

Often, the forces arrayed against the smugglers were too weak to oppose them. Swansea, in South Wales was a hot-bed of activity, and one of the many incidents in this area happened in 1788, when Customs Officers who went to search the home of a gang leader were held at bay by a houseful of men "armed with pokers, iron bars, large knives, loaded whips and other offensive weapons", and an appeal to the Government for troops was refused because of the lack of men.

Again, in 1796, a sergeant and twelve men stood helpless whilst eighteen free-traders of Pwllheli flaunted their contraband as they walked down the streets.

In Scotland the west coast was used extensively for landing contraband which came from Ireland to Galloway and Ayrshire. In 1780 Customs reports from Carlisle stated that a great deal of tea and brandy brought into Scotland was sent over the border to England. Large gangs of free-traders frequented the east coast of Scotland and used to cross the Tees near Barnard Castle.

'Brandy-holes' were plentiful in the district around the Solway and the Firth of Forth, and Mr. Neville Williams in his book *Contraband Cargoes,* says that the uninitiated traveller in 1780 who asked how the local men made a living was told, "We smuggle a little".

As time went on the smugglers became really more businesslike, and a group of free-traders run by Messrs. Christie and Mitchell in Aberdeen advertised gin for sale in 1809 in the *Aberdeen Journal,* which said that it could not be excelled for quality and flavour and that there was "a fresh supply daily expected".

The 'firm' was liquidated in 1817, as a result of the vigilence of the Customs Officers, particularly one called Mr. Arrow, who was known to have kept a smuggling vessel off the coast for thirteen nights or more, and this relentless refusal to allow her to land her cargo caused her to be wrecked, to the dismay of the Aberdeen smugglers.

Some of the dour stolidity of the Scot could have been used to advantage in the Irish Customs organization, for their lax way of running affairs enabled much contraband to enter Ireland without much action being taken by local magistrates — in fact one woman, a Mrs. Fehrman, twice suspected, possibly rightly, of hoarding contraband in her cellar, refused to allow a Customs Officer to search it. She was actually awarded damages of £60 by the local jury.

In County Derry at Cahirciveen, lived a highly skilled organizer of the free-traders whose name was Morgan O'Connell. His son later became a politician, Daniel O'Connell.

The Irish Government lost dues of £200,000 a year through contraband landings at Dublin and "the hydrometer in use, for testing the strength of exported whisky, had not worked for years. Nobody minded".

The lack of strict supervision at the ports did mean that firearms were rarely used, and the gang, whose leader was Jack the Bachelor, had many years of trouble-free smuggling.

In 1801 Union with Great Britain brought heavier dues, and further evasions were made by using illegal stills, particularly in the Counties of Donegal and Tyrone, to make whisky for export. Duty on tobacco from America and Holland was freely evaded, and it was not unusual for the Revenue Cruisers to be bribed to desert their particular station when a run was imminent.

Tobacco companies at New York and Baltimore operated a fleet of vessels to carry their illegal product to Ireland in 1815, and it is interesting to note that during the prohibition era in America the Irish reciprocated by running Irish whisky to America.

Towards the end of the nineteenth century, although the authorities were better able to control smuggling, nevertheless the free-traders continued to have a warm place in the Irish heart.

The Isle of Man was also a hive of smuggling, which provided a livelihood for almost the entire population during the early days of the eighteenth century.

* * * *

Among the special privileges accorded to ambassadors and ministers in London recognised by the British Government in 1707 were the import of clothing, house furnishings and personal effects duty free, and in addition each ambassador was allowed to import a tun, and ministers half a tun, of duty-free wine yearly.

It would appear that some ambassadors and ministers abused their privileges and resorted to downright smuggling. Both the French and Venetian ambassadors were guilty of this offence.

Mr. Williams reports that seized goods at the Venetian Embassy in 1772 were "several hundred chairs, sofas, marble tables, richly gilt frames, silk, lace, tapestry and a ton of curled hair as used by upholsterers", all belonging to Baron Berlendinni — who had set himself up in the furniture trade! The Baron asked for his contraband to be returned to him, but this was refused on the grounds that King George III would not allow his own ministers to infringe the law in Venice and would not permit the Venetian ambassador to do so in this country.

Tea and coffee merchants in London suspected that the Bavarian Minister was secreting contraband goods in his house in 1780. But the Minister, Count Hasland, denying that he had any illicit goods, refused to allow the Customs officers to search his premises. His undoing came some weeks afterwards when his chapel was entered by a mob of Gordon Rioters intending to damage the robes and furniture of the church, and "great quantities of run tea and contraband were found".

The diplomatic bag came under suspicion, for the Dover Customs Officers noticed that the couriers were carrying bigger and bigger bags, and in 1824 a French courier was asked to unlock his bag. Although he denied having the key with him, he was later persuaded to produce a key. In the bag, along with a small portfolio of despatches, was a quantity of contraband.

Almost ten years later Baron de Franchischi brought "silks and blond laces, totally prohibited goods valued at £1,900, in a large portmanteau", and another from the Brazilian Legation was full of jewellery, albeit labelled "Despatches".

The amount of two hundred and fifty two gallons of wine a year which was allowed to the ambassadors to this country was almost always exceeded, and in the early seventeenth century the shipment of wine was supervised more closely. Of 1,074 gallons imported from Spain in 1823, nine hundred and seventy six gallons found their way to the French Embassy and eight hundred and twenty one went to Russia's Count Lieven, all brought in under the care of Admiral Jabel of Spain. In fact the French Ambassador's fourth secretary became a wine merchant in Soho, and in 1834 Customs Officers recorded that

"23 hogsheads, 4 casks, 13 cases, 2 dozen bottles and 12 gallons of wine and 50 bottles of liqueurs had been imported duty-free in the name of Talleyrand, the French Ambassador — about twelve times the authorized quantity."

The Foreign Secretary, then Lord Palmerston, being presented with the statement, observed that it seemed "an enormous quantity of wine for the consumption of one family". It was quite obvious that he realized the full implication of the amount of the goods which were listed.

Mementos which the British Ministers brought from their foreign travel were duty free, but some were regarded with suspicion — especially the 'souvenir' of 726 gallons of Tokay brought in from Vienna by the Marquess of Londonderry in 1823, or the 'curiosities' which were "30 silk dressing gowns from Japan" imported by the Directors of the East India Company.

During 1816 the Controller of the Royal Laboratory at Woolwich, Sir William Congreve, with many others, was involved in a Whig House of Commons Motion which demanded that there should be a public enquiry when packing cases purporting to consist of military supplies were discovered to have other articles in them.

The only interesting outcome of this motion was Cruikshank's intriguing series of cartoons:

"Lace for Ladies Liverpool and Castlereagh" (the wives of the Prime Minister and Foreign Secretary): "Silk Stockings for Lady Derby, mark'd *Bombs*"; "French Brandy for Lady Dickson and Lady Frazer, mark'd *Grape Shot*";

"Snuff boxes with Pretty Pictures in them for Captain Rudyard, mark'd *Stores*"; and "Choice collection of Obscene Books and Prints etc., for the Regiment, sent as Ordnance Stores and mark'd *Bombs* and *Shells*."

25

Bessie Catchpole

AFTER a fierce battle with the revenue men, in which Catchpole, an early nineteenth century free-trader from the East coast, was killed, his wife Bessie took up the trade where he left off and became a daring and resourceful sea-going smuggler in her own right.

She took over her late husband's yawl *Sally* and adopted the male style of dress. The sight of Bessie with a pipe in her mouth and armed with a cutlass provoked ribald laughter from one of her crew, so she promptly struck him on the jaw and knocked him down. From that moment she became the undisputed master of her ship.

She carried out her role with considerable aplomb and success, and appears to have been a skilful smuggling captain without endangering either the lives of her men or her ship.

On one occasion, towards evening, with the wind falling light, a revenue cruiser began to close with her. The wind failed completely, and both ships lay motionless during the night. There was no moon, so she and her crew roped the brandy tubs together, and using sinking stones and a marker, dropped them overboard.

At sunrise the next day the revenue men from the cruiser boarded her and searched the ship from stem to stern, but nothing incriminating could be found. They refused Bessie's hospitable offer of breakfast and made off to their own vessel.

Later, the tubs were recovered and brought on board again, to be landed near Ipswich.

Another time, when she was sailing from Dunkirk to Ipswich with a valuable contraband cargo, and again sighted a revenue cutter, she ran up a large yellow handkerchief and made for the vessel.

The cutter promptly turned and fled, for a yellow flag signalled sickness aboard, and the plague was dreaded by all honest seafaring men.

Bessie certainly had her fair share of fun and luck in evading officers of the revenue cutters, and whilst she continually fooled them, they must have admired her skill in handling her vessel and eluding them. She was a very enterprising sailor, and one of her most successful ruses was to baffle her pursuers by alternating two completely different sets of sails.

No wonder the commander of a revenue cutter once said that to send a cutter after a smuggler was like sending a cow after a hare!

ER THE
PARZON

26

Smugglers Converted

MANY are the free-traders who gave up their wild ways when they became middle aged and prosperous, but there are two outstanding cases on record where men completely changed their ways and devoted their lives to Godly and righteous living.

One of these was 'Captain' Harry Carter, a member of a well known smuggling family from Prussia Cove in Cornwall.

John Wesley visited Cornwall in 1751 and he and his brother Charles were determined to bring a new way of life to the wayward Cornish people. In spite of a hostile reception by the smugglers, who tried to break up their meetings by pelting the preachers with anything they could lay hands on, they persevered with their exhortations to give up the evils of smuggling, and continued their preaching. Gradually all over the area groups of Wesleyan Methodist converts gathered together in meeting houses.

It is obvious from 'Captain' Harry's *Autobiography of a Cornish Smuggler*, that John Wesley's impact on him was considerable.

When one of his adventures led him to New York he there became converted to the Wesleyan Methodist Communion.

His conversion was not achieved without occasional back-sliding, and during the last of his relapses he found himself inside a French Prison during the Reign of Terror. Here the 'spirit' returned upon him and brought comfort to his fellow prisoners among whom were many aristocrats under the shadow of the guillotine.

In 1795, he was liberated and he returned to Cornwall to lead a quiet life on a small farm. He remained a popular and staunch Wesleyan Methodist Preacher for the rest of his life.

Another convert was a dashing young fellow from the Scilly Isles called William Gibson, who thought nothing of rowing 150 miles to France in a small open boat to return with a cargo of contraband brandy.

It was at the height of his success as a smuggler in the year 1820 that a serious young girl by the name of Mary Ann Werry visited St. Mary's in the Scilly Isles. She was the first Missionary of the Bible Christian Group to land there. She came at a time when the island was interested in a revival and the people were anxious to hear good preachers, but they were not prepared to pay the charge of £2 which their usual minister made each time he came, and finally they refused his services at that price.

When the members of the congregation realized that there was a missionary amongst them, although a woman, they asked Mary Werry to preach. She took her text from the first Book of Timothy, Chapter IV, Verse 8:

"For bodily exercise profiteth little; but godliness is profitable unto all things, having promise of the life that now is, and of that which is to come."

So successful was her sermon, and so moved were even the most hardened of her congregation, that penitential tears rolled from their eyes. Among these was William Gibson, who from then on completely changed his ways and became a prominent preacher in the 'Bible Christian' Communion, known as 'Brother Gibson'. He ended his life as a law-abiding fisherman-pilot and remained true to his faith until he died in 1877 at the age of 83.

'Peep tub' and grapple in the Carisbrooke Castle Museum, Isle of Wight.

27

Brandy for the Parson

A STORY has been told of a raw young Irish priest bringing his worldly goods through the Customs at Dover.

The Customs Officer asked him to open his bag, which contained a bottle.

"What's in this bottle?" queried the Officer.

"Oh — Holy Water from Lourdes".

On hearing this reply the officer removed the cork from the bottle.

"Holy Water?" he said sniffing the contents, "this is brandy!"

To which the priest replied,

"The Lord be praised, 'tis a blessed miracle".

Whether this story is true or not, it is certainly true that brandy was one of the commodities which many a cleric —

may it not be told in convocation — was not loathe to receive, or indeed help to smuggle into this country during the late 18th and early 19th centuries, often at a profit to himself, although the poor and needy in many a parish received substantial help from the parson.

The Revd. R. S. Hawker, of Morwenstow, said that when he somewhat diffidently tried to chide his wayward Cornish smuggling parishioners they answered,

"But why should the King tax good liquor? If they must have taxes why can't they tax something else?"

George III's Government certainly did "tax something else" — apart from the innumerable goods which had to pay duties. In 1799 Pitt imposed an Income Tax as a "temporary war measure", and many a venerable parson felt that the taxes, as a whole, were unjust.

Not only was the wayward cleric in this country guilty of smuggling, but also the parson from abroad was liable to try to deceive the customs. A certain clergyman from Minnesota tried to pass through the New York Customs with "silk umbrellas, ladies' underclothing, perfumery and 5,000 cigars". The clerical smuggler had false bottoms to his trunks.

The clever and compassionate parson-smuggler of those days has been immortalised by Russell Thorndyke in his *Dr. Syn* stories. Together with his parish clerk, Mr. Mipps, and other trusted followers he would roam the Romney Marsh as 'The Scarecrow', the smuggler renowned for his leadership, bravery and daring. No one in real need, escaping the press gang or unjust imprisonment, was ever refused sanctuary or help.

The clergy often turned a blind eye to the contraband which lay hidden in the church vestry or vaults, the tops of towers, the church itself, the churchyards and even the tithe barns adjoining the Rectory. The smugglers' maxim was, "Who better than a parson to care for our tubs?".

The willing co-operation of the sexton and clerk in leaving open a vestry door, opening a vault, or in signalling to the smugglers, was evident in many cases.

The Rev. E. K. Elliott of Worthing related that the smuggling clerk of Broadwater used to go up to the top of the church spire, from which there was a magnificent view of the coast, and when he saw that there were no preventive men about he would hoist a flag to signal, 'all clear', and the smugglers would then land their cargo.

Near the Western porch of Worthing Church stand two big tombs, having tops which slide open, and here many kegs were hidden. The vicar recollected that the last run of contraband in that area was in 1855. A few kegs were taken to Charman Dean and buried underground, and these were not discovered by the customs officers.

Old vaults seem to have been a favourite 'haunt' of these earthly spirits, and in 1800 one at Soberton, in Hampshire, near the door of the chancel, used to have a stone which rested on three feet of brickwork. The clerk and an accomplice used to see that it was lifted off when a run of tubs was expected and then replaced. Nowadays the stone is at ground level. Apparently the curate could never discover who commandeered his horse whenever there was a smuggling venture!

The vault by the entrance porch of 'The Smugglers' Church'

at Kinson, Bournemouth was constantly used as a secret hiding place for contraband.

At Owermoigne, in Dorset, where the Rectory is renowned as being Elizabethan in part, having timbers in the dining room from a ship wrecked off Ringstead Bay during the Armada, the Rector had obviously some sympathies with the Owermoigne smugglers, or at least he pretended not to notice them, for it has been suggested that the cellar in the Rectory, and certainly the Church Tower and an orchard lying westward of the Church, were all used to conceal contraband.

Ringstead Bay is completely secluded and was an ideal landing place for smugglers. The Rector of West Stafford, Archdeacon England, certainly appeared to allow his smuggling parishioners to earn a little extra income, for his tithe barn was used to conceal kegs of brandy by the score, all lying quite safely underneath quantities of straw or hay, and occasionally they were stowed in the church belfry.

An ancient thatched house by the name of Vicar's Mead in East Budleigh, Devon used to be a Vicarage. It is reputed to have been built about 1485, and contained secret hiding places, passages and recesses, some of which still exist today. Tradition has it that Sir Walter Raleigh was tutored there by one of the Vicars of East Budleigh and that it was used extensively as a rendezvous by the free-traders.

Two venerable parsons, the Rev. Matthew Mundy, the incumbent between 1741 and 1794, and the Rev. Ambrose Stapleton from 1794-1852, have the reputation of being keen organizers of many smuggling expeditions and landings of cargo close to the Otter Mouth.

The plans were laid for these ventures in the Vicarage Parish Room, which had two secret passages built between the north and south walls.

In one of the rooms in the old Vicarage is a window pane bearing the scratched inscription:

> "Matt. Mundy Vicr.
> Sept. 24
> 1741
>
> A. A. Stapleton Vicar
> 1794."

So these two smuggling clerics, each living in the beneficial air of East Budleigh for many years, and who, no doubt, were renowned for the fine quality of their brandy wine, left something of their lives to posterity. May the windows never be broken!

Not only was brandy acceptable to the parson, but that reverent theologian, Parson Woodeforde, "a truly good as well as 'respectable' man", was obviously addicted to tea, which, incidentally, had been described as being,

> "bad indeed for all other support; being a vain present attempt to supply to the spirits of the mind what is wanting to the strength of the body, but in its lasting effects impairing the nerves and thence equally injuring to the body and the mind."

In spite of the awful consequences of tea drinking, Parson Woodeforde informed us on the 29th March, 1777 that:

> "Andrews the smuggler brought me this night about 11 o'clock a bag of Hyson tea 6 pound weight. He frightened us a little by whistling under the parlour window just as we were going to bed. I gave him some Genoa and paid him for the tea at 10/6 per pound."

Later, in 1786, he was disturbed by a heavy knock on his door, and he found two tubs on his step, one containing gin and the other brandy. It would appear that 'Andrews, the smuggler', was as commonplace as the term 'Andrews the Grocer' might have been.

Parson Dodge was renowned as an eccentric and an exorcist. He lived at Talland in Cornwall, a remote and solitary place with a lonely church close to the sea shore.

The churchyard was extremely convenient for the men of Polperro to use as a store house for contraband waiting to be carted inland under the cover of seaweed, which was used to manure the farmlands.

The churchyard was reputed to be inhabited by 'The Devils of Talland', weird and terrible apparitions which appeared at night and terrified the local people who were at all times superstitious.

Parson Dodge, whose reputation for ridding the area of troublesome spectres was prodigious — being able to banish them to the Red Sea — was called upon to rid the churchyard of the ghosts, but it would seem that the amiable cleric's vicarage was at times renowned as a meeting place for these supernatural creatures, where they could learn what he wished them to do.

One very dark night it so happened that a villager by the name of Uncle Zack Chowne, was returning from an evening with some of his friends when he met a crowd of 'spectres' lurking in the churchyard. Being full of goodwill and ale, instead of greeting the apparitions with *In Nomine Domini* or 'Nummy Dummy' to exorcise them, he insisted that for old time's sake they should join him at a nearby inn.

Instead, he returned home with a black eye — from the smuggling 'ghosties'.

No wonder, then, that the Cornish folk have a Litany which goes:

> "From ghoulies and ghosties and
> Long leggety beasties, and things
> That go bump in the night,
> Good Lord deliver Us."

An interesting interlude of Cornish smuggling was described by the Rev. R. S. Hawker in a little story entitled, *The Light of Other Days*:

"It was a full sea in the evening of an autumn day when a traveller arrived where the road ran along by a sandy beach just above high water mark. The stranger, who was a native of some inland town, and utterly unacquainted with Cornwall and its ways, had reached the brink of the tide just as a landing was coming off.

It was a scene not only to interest a townsman, but to dazzle and surprise. At sea, just beyond the billows, lay the vessel, well moored with anchors at stem and stern. Between the ship and shore, boats, laden to the gunwhale, passed to and fro. Crowds assembled on the beach to help the cargo ashore.

On one hand a boisterous group surrounded a keg with the head knocked in, for simplicity of access to the good cognac, into which they dipped whatsoever vessel came to hand; one man filled his shoe. On the other side they fought and wrestled, cursed and swore.

Horrified at what he saw, the stranger lost all self-command, and oblivious of personal danger, he began to shout,

'What a horrible sight! Have you no shame? Is there no magistrate at hand? Cannot any justice of the peace be found in this fearful country?'

'No, thanks be to God', answered a gruff hoarse voice. 'None within eight miles'.

'Well then', screamed the stranger, 'is there no clergyman about? Does no minister of the parish live among you on this coast?'

'Aye, to be sure there is', said the same deep voice.

'Well, how far off does he live? Where is he?'

'That's he yonder, sir, with the lantern.'

And sure enough, there he stood on a rock and poured, with pastoral diligence, 'the light of other days' on a 'busy' congregation."

Many a parson who would have remonstrated with his congregation found that his clerk or even his churchwarden was, in some way, either financially or actively interested in a bold venture which had recently been successful.

That famous Morwenstow vicar, Mr. Hawker, observed, in a manner seemingly quite unperturbed by the illicit doings of his flock, that his lawless parishioners

"used to rush at some well-known signal to the strand, the small active horses, shaved from forelock to tail, well soaped or greased from head to foot so as to slip easily out of any hostile grasp; and then with a double keg or pack slung on every nag by a simple girth, away went the whole herd, led by some swift well-trained mare, to the inland cave or rocky hole which formed the rendezvous."

The same parson had a smuggler-gardener, who was one of Cruel Coppinger's victims, being kidnapped by him when he was a boy. His name was Tristram Pentire, and, rogue that he was, told many a story to his master.

He related that a gauger by the name of Parminter used to allow the smugglers free reign if they left a bag of gold for him in a rock behind Tidnacombe Cross which was referred to as 'Gauger's Pocket'.

After the smugglers had done this they would go up to Parminter and say,

"Sir, your pocket is unbuttoned". Then the gauger would answer

"Ay ay, my man, but the money's safe enough".

He would then walk over to the cross, pocket the money and the free-traders carried on their unloading unhindered.

During his employment with the vicar, Tristram Pentire on one occasion bribed the sexton, Tom Hokaday, and one Saturday a complete cargo was hidden under the church seats.

On the Sunday morning Pentire said,

> "The parson did wonder at the large congregation; for numbers of them were not regular churchgoers at other times, and if he had known what was going on he could not have preached a more suitable sermon, for it was, 'Be not drunk with wine, wherein is excess', one of his best sermons, but there — it did not touch us, you see, for we never tasted anything but brandy or gin. Ah, he was a dear man, our parson, mild as milk, nothing could ever put him out."

When another Cornish cleric, Parson Trenowth, was in the middle of morning prayer, there was a buzz down by the porch and his congregation began to leave, so the parson shut his book, took off his surplice, and he said to his clerk,

"There is surely something amiss". And so there was. A King's cutter was chasing their ship the *Black Prince*. The congregation gathered to see this episode. When their vessel ran for the dangerous passage at Gull Rock, the revenue cutter sheered off. The congregation then cheered and when all was quiet again the cleric said to them,

"And now my friends, let us return and proceed with Divine Service".

Which they did to the words, "Here beginneth the second lesson".

The Encyclopedia of Wit (1801) tells a story of another vicar who lived on the Cornish coast among the smuggler-wreckers.

During his sermon, he heard a signal, and his congregation started to move from the Church. He checked them and called out, "My brethren, let me entreat you to stay for five words more: " and leaving the pulpit he walked almost to the door of the church, and said, "Let us all start fair".

* * * *

If you wake at midnight, and hear a horse's feet,
Don't go drawing back the blind, or looking in the street—
Them that asks no questions isn't told a lie.
Watch the wall, my darling. While the Gentlemen go by!

Five and twenty ponies,
Trotting through the dark—
Brandy for the Parson,
'Baccy for the Clerk;
Laces for a Lady; letters for a spy;
And watch the wall, my darling, while the Gentlemen go by!

A Smuggler's Song,
by Rudyard Kipling.

Christchurch Priory
Church

ACKNOWLEDGEMENTS

My grateful thanks for valuable help, advice and documents are extended to:

Mr. John Macfadyen, D.F.C., LL.B. The Town Clerk of Christchurch, Hampshire.

Sir Donald Bailey, O.B.E., J.P.

The Revd. Leslie Yorke, L.Th., Vicar of the Priory Church, Christchurch.

The Revd. Canon W. E. Norris, Romsey Abbey.

Mr. J. H. Lavender, B.Sc., A.R.C.S., Curator of The Red House Museum, Christchurch.

Mrs. R. Lavender, B.A., Bransgore.

Mr. R. H. Clarke, A.R.A., Librarian, Christchurch Library.

Mr. G. H. Watson, President of the Wimborne Museum, Dorset.

Mr. M. Case, Reference Library, Bournemouth.

Mr. J. T. Beattie, H.M. Officer of Customs and Excise, Christchurch.

Mr. J. Rothwell, H.M. Officer of Customs and Excise, Poole, Dorset.

Dr. R. H. Little, Ringwood, Hampshire.

The British Museum.

Mr. G. Naish and Miss P. Sichel, The National Maritime Museum, Greenwich.

Mr. Donovan Lane, Christchurch.

Mr. G. G. Mapp, F.L.A.S., Bournemouth.

Miss V. J. Thornton, Mudeford, Hampshire.

R. Vigar, Esq., Winton.

Mr. A. T. Lloyd, B.A., Barton-on-Sea.

Group Captain S. C. George, Highcliffe, Christchurch.

The Archivist of the Admiralty Library, London.

The Librarian, The War Office, London.

The Civil Engineer-in-Chief, Admiralty, Pinner, Middlesex.

Mr. David Brackston, Bournemouth.

Ald. E. Spreadbury, Friars Cliff, Christchurch.

Miss F. G. Hamilton, Mudeford.

Mr. A. L. Slater, LL.B. Town Clerk of Lymington.

Mrs. George Bambridge and Messrs. Macmillan & Co. Ltd., for their kind permission to reproduce the verses from *A Smuggler's Song* and *Poor Honest Men* by Rudyard Kipling, and to the following for their kind permission to quote from the works mentioned:

Messrs. Hutchinson, *The Smugglers of Christchurch, Bourne Heath, and the New Forest,* by E. Russell Oakley.

Mr. E. King of Lymington, *Boldre,* by W. F. Perkins.

Messrs. Longmans, Green & Co., *English Social History,* by G. M. Trevelyan.

Messrs. Methuen & Co. Ltd., *In Search of England,* by H. V. Morton.

Captain J. R. W. Coxhead, *Smuggling Days in Devon,* published by The Raleigh Press, Exmouth.

Mrs. K. S. Jellis, *Back of the Wight,* published by the Isle of Wight County Press.

Neville Williams, Esq., *Contraband Cargoes,* published by Longmans, Green & Co. Ltd.

B. A. Mead, Esq., B.Com. Editor, *Christchurch Times, Sophy the Winkle Picker,* by the Hon. Mrs. Stuart Wortley, C.B.E

Oliver Warner, Esq., *Captain Marryat, A Rediscovery,* published by Constable, London.

Messrs. Ward, Lock & Co. Ltd., *At War With The Smugglers,* by Rear-Admiral D. Arnold Forster.

Miss F. Hardcastle, *Records of Burley.*

Messrs. George Allen & Unwin Ltd., *King's Cutters and Smugglers,* by E Keble Chatterton.

Mr. Allen White, Christchurch historian.

BIBLIOGRAPHY

PRIMARY MATERIAL

Original letter from Captain Marryat to the Admiralty.
Records of a Riding Officer of Customs and Excise 1803-1804.
Documents in the possession of the Town Clerk of Christchurch for 1823, 1845, 1846, 1857.
Christchurch Cartulary 1372, British Museum.
Extract from a survey of the Manor of Hinton Admiral, the Hundred of Christchurch and Westover, 1782.
Documents in Romsey Abbey 1795.
Plans of the original Christchurch Barracks.
Reminiscences of 1800 by George Saunders.
Letters from the War Office Library. } Personal
Letters from the Admiralty. } Personal
Parish Registers of Christchurch Priory Church.

SECONDARY MATERIAL

A Shepherd's Life, by W. H. Hudson. Published by Methuen & Co. Ltd.
Buckler's Hard, by Lord Montagu of Beaulieu. Published by Pitken Specials, London.
The Autobiography of a Cornish Smuggler, 1749-1809. Published by Cornish, 1894.
Back of the Wight, by F. Mew. Published by the County Press, Newport, 1951.
Encyclopedia Brittanica, 9th Edition. Published by Adam & Charles Black, Edinburgh.
Footprints of Former Men in Far Cornwall, by Rev. R. S. Hawker. Printed by the Wessex Press, Somerset.
Smuggling Days in Devon, by J. R. W. Coxhead. Published by The Raleigh Press, Exmouth, 1956.
The East Coast Smugglers, by Harvey Benham. Published in "Yachts and Yachting", 1963.
Boldre, by Frank Perkins. Published by King's Library, Lymington, 1935.
Contraband, by W. H. Cooke-Yarborough. Printed by Ralph & Brown, Parkstone c., 1914.
Smuggling Days in Purbeck, by W. M. Hardy.
Records of Burley, by F. Hardcastle. Published by Raleigh Press, Devon.
The Island Race, by Winston S. Churchill. Published by Cassell, London, 1964.

Up Along, Down Along, Edited by Marianne R. Dacomb. Published by Dorset Federation of Women's Institutes.
New Forest, by Horace G. Hutchinson. Published by Methuen & Co. Ltd., London.
It Happened in Hampshire, compiled and arranged by W. G. Beddington & E. B. Christy. Published by Hampshire Federation of Women's Institutes.
Tales of the Hundred of Ford. Printed by A. H. King, Fordingbridge, 1928.
A Guide to the New Forest, by Heywood Sumner, F.S.A. Published by Charles Brown & Son, Ringwood.
Smuggling Days and Smuggling Ways, by H. N. Shore. Published by Cassell, 1892.
Smugglers of Christchurch, Bourne Heath and the New Forest, by Russell Oakley. Published by Hutchinson, 1944.
Cornish Seafarers, by A. K. H. Jenkin. Published by Dent, 1932.
The Smugglers, Volumes I, II, by Lord Teignmouth and Charles G. Harper. Published by Cecil Palmer.
Contraband Cargoes, by Neville Williams. Published by Longmans, 1959.
English Social History, by G. M. Trevelyan. Published by Longmans, Green & Co. Ltd., 1942.
Portrait of Dorset, by Rena Gardiner. Published by "Workshop Press", Wareham, Dorset, 1960.
The Parish Clerk, by P. H. Ditchfield. Published by Methuen & Co., 1907.
Highways and Byways in Devon and Cornwall, by A. Norway. Published by Macmillan & Co., 1897.
At War with the Smugglers, by Rear Admiral Arnold Forster. Published by Ward Lock & Co., 1936.
Compleat Smuggler, by Jefferson Farjeon. Published by George G. Harrap & Co. Ltd., London, 1938.
Tales of Lulworth in Olden Days, by J. and P. Loader. Printed by J. Looker, 82 High Street, Poole.
The Dorset Bedside Anthology, compiled by Margaret Goldsworthy. Published by Billings & Sons Ltd., Guildford & Esher, 1951.
The Royal Malady, by Charles Chenevix Trench. Published by Longmans, 1964.
Captain Thos. Johnstone, by James Cleugh. Published by Andrew Melrose Ltd., 1955.
The History of Christchurch, by Taylor Dyson. Printed by Henbest Publicity Service, Bournemouth.
Chronicles of the Customs, by W. D. Chester, 1885.
History of Poole, by John Sydenham. Published by Whittaker & Co., London, 1839.
Once Upon a Tide, by Hervey Benham. Published by Harrap, 1955.

Memoirs of a Smuggler, by Jack Rattenbury. Published by J. Harvey, Sidmouth.
The Kings Customs, Volume I by H. Atton & H. Hurst Holland. Published by John Murray, London, 1908.
The Organisation of the English Customs System, by E. E. Hoon. Published by Appleton-Century Co. Ltd., New York, London, 1938.
Sophy the Winkle Picker, by the Hon. Mrs. Stuart Wortley, C.B.E. Published by The Christchurch Times, 1930.
Captain Marryat, A Rediscovery, by Oliver Warner. Published by Constable, London, 1953.
The Hampshire Repository, Volumes I and II, 1798, 1799.
The Christchurch Miscellany.
Salisbury Journal, 1757-58-59.
Reminiscences of Christchurch, by Wm. Tucker. Printed by the Christchurch Times c., 1921.
The Story of Bournemouth, by David S. Young. Published by Robert Hale Ltd., London, 1957.
Dr. Syn, by Russell Thorndyke. Published by Rich & Cowan, 1915.
Black's Guide to Hampshire. Published by Adam and Charles Black, 1881.
Kings Cutters and Smugglers, by E. Keble Chatterton, Published by George Allen & Co. Ltd., 1912.
In Search of England, by H. V. Morton. Published by Methuen & Co. Ltd., 1927.
Literary Recollections, by Rev. Richard Warner. Published by Longman, Rees, Orme, Brown & Green, 1830.
Old Times Revisited, by Edward King, 2nd Edition, Published 1900.

INDEX

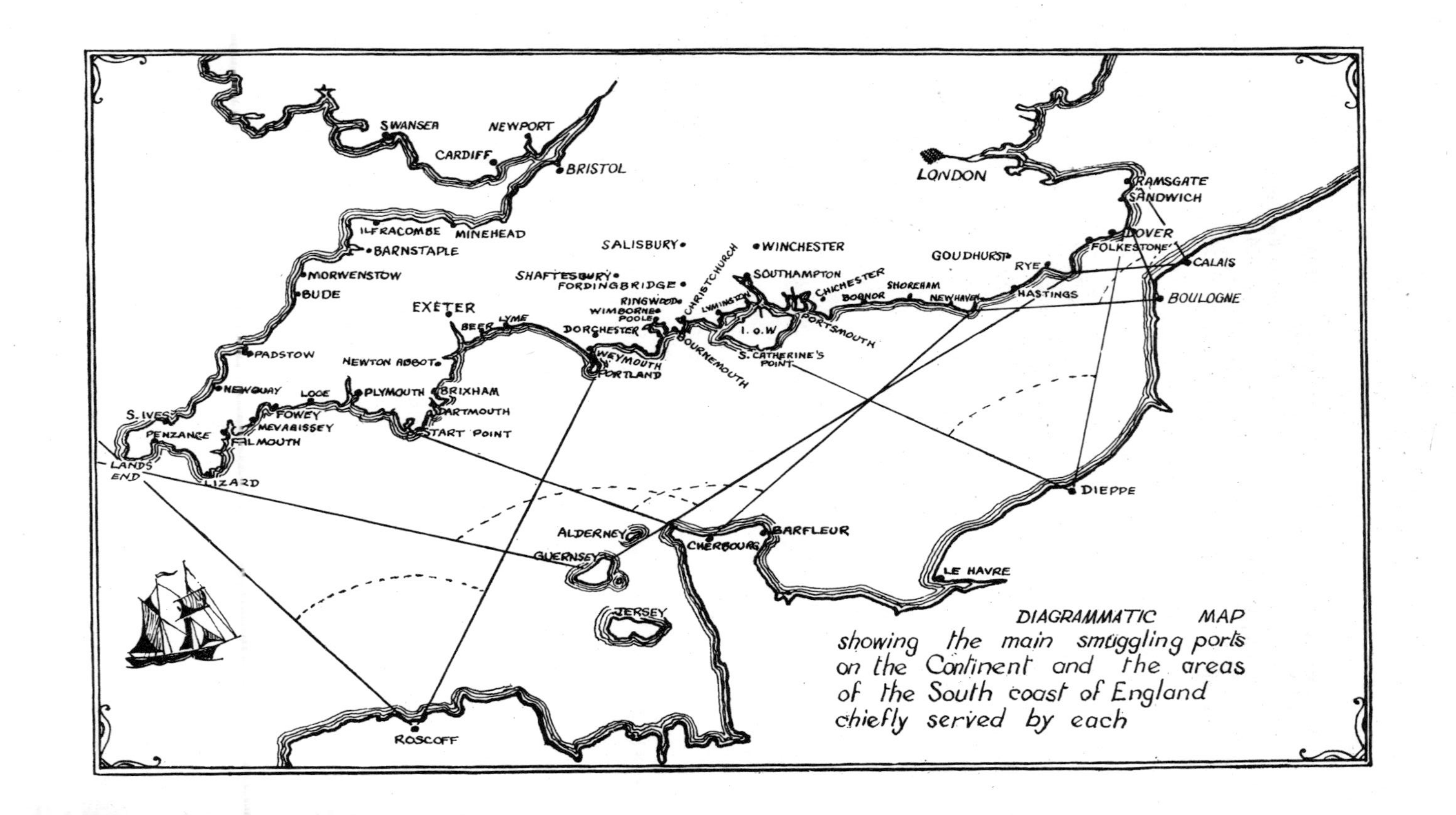
SWANSEA
NEWPORT
CARDIFF
BRISTOL
LONDON
RAMSGATE
SANDWICH
DOVER
FOLKESTONE
CALAIS
BOULOGNE
ILFRACOMBE
MINEHEAD
BARNSTAPLE
MORWENSTOW
BUDE
SALISBURY
WINCHESTER
SHAFTESBURY
FORDINGBRIDGE
CHRISTCHURCH
SOUTHAMPTON
CHICHESTER
GOUDHURST
RYE
SHOREHAM
BOGNOR
NEWHAVEN
HASTINGS
RINGWOOD
WIMBORNE
POOLE
LYMINGTON
EXETER
BEER
LYME
DORCHESTER
I. O. W
PORTSMOUTH
S. CATHERINE'S POINT
PADSTOW
NEWTON ABBOT
WEYMOUTH
PORTLAND
BOURNEMOUTH
NEWQUAY
LOOE
PLYMOUTH
BRIXHAM
DARTMOUTH
S. IVES
FOWEY
MEVAGISSEY
PENZANCE
FALMOUTH
START POINT
LANDS END
LIZARD
DIEPPE
ALDERNEY
BARFLEUR
CHERBOURG
GUERNSEY
LE HAVRE
JERSEY
ROSCOFF
DIAGRAMMATIC MAP
showing the main smuggling ports
on the Continent and the areas
of the South coast of England
chiefly served by each